Published by Rhythm Knight Publishing
Ft. Lauderdale, FL

Printed in the United States of America
First Edition
Library of Congress Cataloging-in-Publication Data
Knight, T. Rhythm
Diary of a Basketball Mom
ISBN-978-1-257-97603-4

Diary Of A
Basketball
Mom

For Brandon – you are perfect in every way.
I love you to pieces….

God chooses people to do all kinds things…I thank Him
for choosing me to be your mom.

Acknowledgements

First and above all else, I have to thank God for giving me the gift of writing.

Secondly, I'd like to thank Paul Dick. Every once in a while God sends an angel. This time it was Paul. Although I've seen him walking in the hallways of our building many times, I had no clue that he was an editor. One day I mentioned I was writing a book; Paul offered to help with the editing… it was as simple as that. Paul, I will forever be grateful for your patience and kindness.

To my Lexington crew on hot Roosie…I love you all. Thanks for all of the love and support you guys have shown me since I've been in Lexington. To Efrem, thanks for keeping the facts straight, your attention to detail is amazing!

Next, to the BIG BLUE NATION…I've never seen fans like you. Your passion and love of your team inspired me to write this book, to you, I'll forever be grateful. GO BIG BLUE!

Finally, to Coach Cal….you and I may not have seen eye-to-eye on everything but you got Brandon where he wanted to be—the NBA. For that, I thank you. Best wishes on the upcoming season!

In the Beginning

(November 2000)

Rec League
Today, we went to Firefighter's Park for Brandon's basketball tryouts. I sure am nervous for him. I'm nervous because he seems to think he can really play basketball. Can he? Don't ask me. What do I know? Not much, except for this one simple fact: he does a mighty fine job of dribbling the ball through his legs while walking (I find that quite interesting). He also does a fine job of bouncing the ball up and down our driveway (much to our neighbors dismay), but can he play? I don't know. We shall see soon enough.

The Day After Tryouts
Yesterday, the people at the park looked impressed while watching Brandon. I couldn't tell if they were impressed-impressed, or if they, like I, thought he did a mighty fine job of dribbling the ball through his legs while walking! Apparently, they were truly impressed. His dad just brought him back from the park where they saw Brandon's name on the list of kids who made the team! Wow! They even gave him a uniform – uh, maybe I should say a t-shirt with a Miami Heat logo ironed on it. I think we're responsible for getting him the rest of his uniform: a pair of black shorts. Ha!

Unlike Brandon's football games, I will definitely attend the basketball games. (I really felt bad about not going to

1

the football stuff, but I HATE football! What can I say?!?)

Can't wait for the first game. Should be fun!

Rec League 101 (January 2001)
Quite a few games have rolled on since my first entry, and I'm learning how this thing called "Rec League Ball" works. First of all, all kids must participate. Even if the kid sucks (sorry) and will cause you to lose, that kid will play! Huh? There's one kid on the team who would probably be better off staying home and working on his science project because basketball is clearly not his thing. I wonder why parents do this? Surely, they know their kid isn't cut out for athletics! I know this because they put their heads down and let out gut-wrenching moans every time their kid touches the ball. These poor kids are mortified, too! One kid looked like he'd rather be at Gatorland playing with alligators than running up and down the court! And the coaches are no better. They're running around with pasted smiles on their faces which say, "I'm smiling, but I really want to hire somebody to take this kid and hold him hostage in the bathroom until the game is over."

I know, I know … I'm bad. But hey, I've got problems too! It turns out that Brandon is too good to play. They actually make him sit the bench! Who ever heard of such a thing??? They say he runs the score up too much when he's in the game and that it's really unfair to have the score 30 – 2. I suppose they're right, but try telling an 8-year-old boy that he can't play because he's too good. It just doesn't fly! My heart breaks as I look at him sitting on the bench crying because he can't play. But on the flip side, when the team starts to lose, the coaches want to let Brandon in the game. I'm getting EXTREMELY heated …I'm mad. I mean, don't use the baby to bring you back in the game when you fool around and let the opposing team out score you!!! To make matters worse, Efrem (his dad, my husband) is getting heated, too! And the last thing anyone wants is for Efrem to act a fool. Trust me, it won't be pretty!

For now, we'll shut up and deal with this until Brandon tells us he doesn't want to play. But I know he won't want to stop playing because he's becoming quite the athlete.

Surprise Visit

It's midway through the season, and things are pretty much the same. Brandon doesn't play the whole quarter even though he should (according to the rules). The rules state five kids play the first quarter, and then another five play the second quarter, and after halftime, they repeat the same rotation. Brandon plays, but not the whole quarter. The other day he got in the game and scored a quick ten points. After only a couple of minutes in the game, guess what? He found himself sitting on the bench a couple of minutes into the quarter, once again. Tension is growing, but I keep reminding myself that the season is almost over.

About a week ago, some teenager who plays on the rec league's 17-year-old team came and introduced himself

3

to us. He said his name was J.R., and apparently, J.R. was at Brandon's game that day to watch him play. You see, J.R. thought there was some kind of discrepancy on the league's stat sheets and was at the game to check things out. It turns out that J.R. has forever been the league's high scorer – that is, up until now because Brandon has officially replaced him (even though Brandon's not being played for a full quarter!) J.R. decided to come check things out and to see for himself because he thought the stats guy was playing a trick on him. After J.R. watched Brandon pull a 12-point run, J.R. shook his head and walked away. Better luck next year, J.R.!

The Main Event

(March 2001)

Tournament time is upon us. There's a kid by the name of Kenny who plays on the opposing team, and word is that Kenny is the cream of the crop in the world of rec league ball, and EVERYONE is talking about the "Great Kenny." As Efrem and I approached the park, I realized I'd never seen so many people. There were people everywhere! Surely, they were not there to watch an 8-year-old-boys rec league basketball tournament? But after a little investigative work, I found out that they surely were! And what's more, everybody was dying to see a Brandon/Kenny showdown!

As I walked closer to the court, a woman swaggered up to me and said, "I'm Kenny's mom." Then she eyed me

4

up and down and walked away…long eyelashes, tight jeans, high-heels and all. Lady, please! You ain't Michael Jordan's mom! In fact, this woman is strutting around with more swagger than Michael Jordan himself! "Kick his butt, Brandon," I mumbled as this chick swished away!

At the half Brandon and Kenny were trading shots like gunfire at a cowboy fight. Brandon won the battle and the Kenny crowd was completely silent. And guess what? The coach didn't sit Brandon down at all during the game! I became more heated because I realized the coach was using MY boy to make HIMSELF look good! Humph! I decided that I definitely had to have a talk with him after the game 'cause I was fired up!

Well anyway, Brandon outscored Kenny by 15 points, and we won the game! Kenny's mom just walked past me and rolled her eyes! Funny, I didn't see that swagger anymore! She looked beat up AND beat down. Secretly I said, "YOU GO BRANDON!" Next, I had to go fry bigger fish: the coach!

After telling the coach to either let Brandon play the same amount of time as he lets the other kids play and NOT only play him when he needs him, the coach looked at me and said, "It's not all about Brandon." What?!? You know those electric machines that fire out basketballs to players during practice? I wish I had one of those because I would have aimed it right at that coach's head and set it on high! IS HE SERIOUS?! It's "about Brandon" when he wants to win a game! I felt like a boiling teapot about to explode as I stood in front of him! Uggh!!! And to make matters worse, Efrem was just as heated as I. I can't be sure, but I think they threatened to remove Efrem from the park if he didn't calm down. I know they told me I would be removed if I didn't stop! Ha! This is crazy. This is rec league ball. This is a bunch of 8-year-old boys! I CAN'T BELIEVE IT HAS COME TO THIS!

There has to be someplace else for Brandon to play ...

Where Will We Go?
It's been a couple of weeks since the rec league fiasco, and as I look back on the whole thing, I have the feeling that I should probably be ashamed. But I'm not. If they can follow the rules when a kid is terrible and let them play two quarters per game, they should do the same when a kid is good. I had no idea Brandon could actually play! Even though he's only 8 years old, I got a feeling that he's going to be somebody special. Am I suffering from PMS: "Proud Mama Syndrome?" Probably, but if it's his dream to go to the NBA, it has to be mine, too. There's only one problem now: where will he play? The park is out. Maybe there's another park out there somewhere ... Oh well, guess we'll have to do some research when rec league season begins again.

The Jammers Year One

(March 2001)

Just in Time

It's been about a week since my last entry. Today, we received some great news. Out of the blue, this fella knocked on our door. His name is Andrew, and Andrew has a son who goes to school with Brandon. Andrew says his son told him Brandon can really play basketball, so he stopped by to talk with Efrem. Guess what? Andrew coaches a travel league team called the Jammers and wants Brandon to join! What's a travel league team and what do they do? I haven't a clue. Efrem seems excited, so I guess I'll be excited, too.

On a different note, Andrew's hair is so red that from a distance, it looks like his head is on fire! Ha!

Practice, Practice, Practice

It's been two weeks since Andrew knocked on our door. Travel basketball is a whole different animal than rec basketball. For starters, they don't care if the score is 102 – 2, if you can play—YOU WILL PLAY!!

When I first saw all of the kids playing on the team, I shook my head in dismay. Now, don't get me wrong. I'm not saying they're Bad-News-Bears bad … well, yes, I am. There's a couple of kids that might be able to

7

play, but I don't think we're going to fair well for the season.

One thing is for sure, they sure have some jazzy looking uniforms! Andrew has a coaching partner, and they run a pretty tight ship. No t-shirt with an iron-on logo here. So, if the kids can't play, they will at least look like they can!

Brandon is so excited. He's been practicing his little heart out. But as with everything, there are pros and there are cons. Dad has already spelled out the cons:

1. As soon as we see grades slip, basketball will be a thing of the past.
2. As soon as anything less than 100% is given, basketball will be a thing of the past.
3. Any disrespectfulness towards coaches, refs, or other players, well, you guessed it!

First Tournament (April 2001)

We won. Huh? We won! I'm shocked ... the other team is shocked ... the Jammer parents are shocked ... and even our own kids look shocked!! I knew I wasn't being awful when I said they were Bad-News-Bears bad, guess what? One of the parents told me they were called "The Bad News Jammers!" Umph!

The first team we played came out like they were going to beat us down, and their coach reminded me of a rooster with his chest puffed out before they even blew the first whistle. I guess he was strutting his stuff based on years of kicking some Jammer butt. Funny thing is that after trailing by 15 points in the first quarter, his chest ended up looking more like a teacup Chihuahua's than that of a prized-rooster!

To win the trophy, we had to beat out four teams, and by the time we beat the second team, kids from the two remaining teams sat in the stands looking at Brandon like he was Lebron or somebody. Brandon averaged 28 points for the tournament and received the MVP trophy!

The Agony of Defeat (Summer 2001)

The season's moving on, and the competition is getting tougher. Today, we played in a tournament in Orlando. This team came out on us and went to work. They wasted no time running up the score. PROBLEM: The second we began to trail, Brandon had a complete meltdown. I'm talking dribbling up and down the court crying meltdown. If there's one thing I know, it's this: BRANDON IS A SORE LOSER. This is nothing new. This is a carryover from his football days. He hates to lose, and so do we. Only difference is Efrem and I can hide our emotions a little better than Brandon can. And speaking of Brandon, we've reached a conclusion regarding his meltdowns: don't feed into it. We've learned that the more you feed into it, the worse it gets.

We lost the game, and of course, Brandon went into meltdown overdrive. While the other kids ate hot dogs and had a good time, Brandon sat in a corner crying. Some lady came to me and said, "Who's that little boy crying?" I told her I didn't know! Of course, I felt like an idiot when she saw him get into the car with us. Ha!

***

Fortunately, it only takes a day for Brandon to return to normal. Thank goodness he doesn't stay mad for long. After last week's loss, things returned to normal pretty quickly, that is until today. This weekend was nationals, and since nationals are held in Cocoa Beach this year, Efrem and I didn't attend due to work commitments. But Brandon went, and one of the parents, Sonya, volunteered to watch over him since we couldn't be there. Around six o'clock today, Sonya gave us a call. Uh oh! Apparently, they lost and were moved to the consolation bracket. Sonya also called to tell us that Brandon informed them (tears and all) that he didn't want to play in the consolation bracket! Thank God Sonya is a tough customer and didn't put up with that garbage. She told us that she told him to go dry up his tears and get ready to play since there's no choice in the matter. Brandon simply looked at her and said, "Ok." She said he came out of the bathroom, got on the court, and performed like the true warrior that he is.

Telling Brandon to stop crying over losses or that it's just a game really doesn't seem to do any good. I'm concerned about the meltdowns. His teacher called me in to tell me that Brandon is brilliant but on the occasions when she has to correct him, he has a meltdown. I know this is true because homework time has become a nightmare in our home. Brandon is a perfectionist and just wants to do everything right. I had a talk with Efrem today and Efrem's response was this, "I fail to believe Brandon will be running around on the court and in class crying when he's in high school. He'll be just fine." Hmph, we'll see!

Speaking of Efrem (who's usually a pretty quiet person), he's become the official "Yeller at the refs." Oh my God, it's so bad that I don't even bother to sit near him during games! The officials threaten to kick him out of the gym quite often. But if there's one thing to be said about him, it's this: Efrem doesn't discriminate. He has been threatened with getting kicked out of the best gyms (Disney) and the worst gyms (most middle school gyms) in Florida.

The Jammers Year Two

(Summer 2002)

Friends and enemies

I can't believe it's been a year and some change since Brandon started travel basketball. So much has changed, yet so much has stayed the same. For starters, Andrew is no longer a coach. A couple of weeks ago, he came to the team and said the game of basketball has passed his son by (I really respect him for realizing and admitting it) – and because of that, they've decided to concentrate on baseball. But Andrew is our neighbor, and since he thinks Brandon could beat Michael Jordan any day of the week (even though Brandon is only 11), he regularly comes to Brandon's games to cheer him on.

Brandon hasn't changed concerning the occasional meltdown either, and it looks like coaches on the opposing teams have caught on to that and are telling their kids to get inside Brandon's head in order to really set him off. Another unchanging fact is Efrem and the yelling at the refs. Every time they make what he deems an unfair call, it's on like buttered popcorn!

Somewhere along the line we've all become fierce competitors (notice I didn't say sore losers). When we lose, all of us claim some kind of cheating was going on!

Brandon continues to be the high scorer on the team, which has caused a host of parents to not really care for us simply because Brandon can play basketball. Yeah, yeah, yeah, they smile to our faces, but then they make slick comments when they think we're not listening. *"They think Brandon is all that!" "Brandon can't win all by himself!" "Why doesn't the coach ever yell at Brandon?"* I'm learning that basketball games are not just a fun thing that parents bring their kids to the gym to do. It's way more than that. It's an unspoken contest as to whose kid is better. One thing I find interesting is this: When people see Brandon's athletic abilities, they are quick to say, *"Yeah, but my kid is really smart in school."* Am I being nasty when I say, "Brandon has earned straight A's since starting school, and he's a genius?" Probably, but my mother always said, "If you start a battle, be prepared for a war!"

The parents on the other teams are starting to say Brandon is not 11. They think he's older and that we pulled some fishy business to get him to play on a younger team. And because of that foolishness, I've started keeping copies of Brandon's report cards in my purse. When those parents start talking that age nonsense, I whip out a report card, shove in their face, and if they have any brains in their head at all, they'll figure out quick enough that a kid who earns straight A's has not been held back in school and is therefore playing with kids his own age! Of course, none of those "age" assumptions are based on anything other than Brandon's skill level. I don't want to brag, but he's seriously beyond his years when it comes to playing this game!

Despite it all, we do have some friends on the team. Two sets of parents have been awesome. I guess you can't help but bond with someone when you go through as many battles as we have. Wins, losses, cuts, bruises, and even broken bones! Being a basketball mom is not easy, but when you love your son and want the best for him, then it's not hard either.

The Jammers Year Three

(Summer 2003)

We've added a lot of pieces to our little team. We are playing very well and have won three state championships so far.

Today we played a team from North Carolina in the Disney tournament. They have managed to go undefeated for two years! When they walked in the gym they pretty much acted like they owned it. They looked at our team like we were nothing! The funny thing is this...although we don't look big and bad, we have secret weapons. One kid is the size of a toothpick but if you can get him the ball when he's set, he's knocking down a three. Another kid, Matt, has got to be the toughest defender playing AAU basketball these days. Matt is tough and he's not backing down from anybody. Another contributing factor to our wins is the fact that several of our kids are fundamentally sound and therefore make good decisions when they have the ball. Then we have Chris. Chris is very fast and can break away easily. Brandon sees the court well and can get Chris the ball when he's ahead of the crowd (which accounts for a lot of our points). Finally, there's Brandon. Brandon is Brandon, what can I say? He's got all kinds of bows in his quiver. Anyway, I digress; back to the Carolina team...this team was shell-shocked when they got their beat down! They were handed down their first lost in a couple of years, today. Brandon averaged

31 points during the tournament and got the MVP trophy again.

***

Today we played in a tournament in Jupiter, Florida. As we were in McDonalds, a team came in and noticed that we were the Jammers. About three or four of the kids wanted to know where Brandon Knight was because they "heard" he was the #1 player in the nation. One of the kids looked at Brandon and said, "Hey man, where's Brandon Knight?" I cracked up when Brandon looked at the kid, hunched his shoulders, and said, "I don't know." Brandon hates attention. All he wants to do is play and win, forget about the fame that goes along with it a kid in elementary school.

***

This year has been a great AAU season. I am, however, anxiously awaiting Junior High. We've done a lot of traveling this year and we've been winning a lot of games. I'm proud of all of our kids and can't wait to see what next year brings!

Ramblewood - Junior High Year One

(2003 – 2004 School Year)

Mr. Big

Mr. Brandon thinks he's a big boy now that he's in junior high school. Today was his first try out for his school's team at Ramblewood. He looked so cute riding his bike home from practice. I asked him how did he do, and he said he did well. I'm sure he'll make the team, but he looks a little apprehensive nonetheless.

Onward and Upward

Brandon just informed me that he made the junior high school team! I can't wait to see him play in his first school setting. From what I'm told, there are only going to be six games, but so what? I'm sure it's going to be fun and exciting. I'm anxious to see if Efrem will yell at the refs for bad officiating in junior high like he did during the Jammers games. Please, please let it not be so. Efrem, like Brandon, is a perfectionist, and he probably (notice I said "probably") sees every call. Unfortunately, everyone doesn't possess the same hawk eye as he does. This causes him major stress, and he doesn't hesitate to let everyone know what a poor job the refs are doing. It's funny because people think he's a lunatic until they talk to him. Once they get to know him, they all say the same thing, "Mr. Knight, you're one of the nicest people I've ever met. I really thought you were different!" In any event, I don't plan on breaking tradition. I will continue my practice of not sitting anywhere near him. Ha!

Who is That Kid?

"Who is that kid?" It seems every coach that we've played against has asked that question. Just because we're in the suburbs, everyone thinks there's no way a "baller" can be on the team. That being said, up until now, Ramblewood was never considered competition. Now that Brandon is on the team, Ramblewood has become a force to be reckoned with! Consequently, everyone wants to know, WHO'S THAT KID?

It's funny to sit in the bleachers and listen to the comments of other parents. Since there's only one set of bleachers on one side of the gym at Brandon's school, there's no choice but to mingle ... and to listen to unsolicited comments. Everyone swears Brandon has been held back a year because he's more skilled and taller than most of the other kids. Granted he's a few months older than a lot of the kids in his class, but that's only because his birthday is in December, and he couldn't start school until the fall after he turned six. Consequently, Brandon turned 7 in December in the first grade, and most other kids turned 7 after the first of the year. If those couple of months make him that detrimental to the game of basketball, these parents should be writing the state of Florida! My personal favorite was yesterday. These people sat behind me and claimed Brandon wasn't even in Ramblewood's school district. They said the school is allowing the parents (us) to forge an address so that he can play for the school. Most of the time I just sit there and listen, but on this particular occasion, I had to whip out my driver's license to show them that we live a couple of blocks away from the school. Talk about an awkward moment (for them).

Game Over

Just like that, the season ended. We made it to the championship but lost. It was a great year, and we beat some teams that nobody thought possible. It was only a six-game season, but it was cool – cheerleaders and all! Andrew made it to quite a few games. You gotta love Andrew…he swears Brandon is ready for the NBA already.

The Jammers Year Four

(Summer 2004)

12 Year-Old Nationals

Another year of AAU basketball has passed, and we're at the nationals in Virginia Beach. The opening ceremony gave me chills, seriously. Teams from all over the country are here. When they announced the teams one by one, I was in awe. Some of these teams have really nice uniforms. But I must say...our little Jammers weren't looking shabby either!

Even though we're playing in Virginia Beach, we're staying in Williamsburg. It's about an hour-long commute one way. We had to do it because the hotels in Virginia Beach were outrageous in price. Most parents couldn't afford $200.00 rooms. One of the parents is really good at organizing and she came up with a solution. She and her sister have timeshares. They used their timeshare points to acquire two three bedroom condos. A couple of days ago I had it out with the parent that did all of the organizing because she had something slick to say about Brandon. I temporarily forgot I was living with her for the week. I felt like a fool when we arrived back to our living quarters and I had to sit down and eat with her. Oh well, such is the life of a basketball mom!

***

Each game brings about a certain nervousness. The kids are physically enormous, and the competition is unlike anything we've seen from the teams we've played in Florida. So far, we've been hanging pretty well (we've been here three days and we've beat four teams). There are over 100 teams here, and only one will win the championship. Let's see what tomorrow brings.

***

Oh Noooo!
Today sucked! We lost! We didn't lose by much, but we lost! Of course, according to the Knight family, THERE WAS SOME CHEATING GOING ON! Brandon found a corner and had another one of his now famous meltdowns. I will have a talk with him because opposing coaches are still trying to use that against him. The good thing is that even though Brandon gets upset, he still plays hard and continues to rack up points.

On another note, word concerning Brandon has spread! There were all kinds of coaches and internet sport writers at our game today. Everyone is talking about how well he played, and we've been approached by several teams to let him play for them. Shipping him off during the summer to play on somebody's team is not our style, so that's out. Everyone has been telling us that we're hurting Brandon by leaving him on the Jammer team. Hey, we're loyal, and we just don't want to make a decision too quickly. In the end, we do know that we have to do what's best for Brandon. Decisions, decisions, decisions.

After our loss the parents and the team went out to dinner. There's this kid on the team who has about ten siblings (seriously). Well, as we were about to leave the gym this little fella (about five years-old) was crying over in the corner while clutching his Game Boy for dear life. I recognized him and as it turns out the colossal family forgot one! We scooped the little fella up and reunited him with his family when we got to the restaurant. His parents were mortified. The mother swore she did a head count. I told her not to feel bad. If I had ten or eleven children, someone would definitely get left behind too. It hurts my head to even think about it. Anyway, all's well that ends well!

***

Since we're stuck in Virginia Beach for a few days, we decided to attend the finals. T.G. Adidas Express is in the finals (along with their obnoxious coach). They've won the championship two or three times in a row so far. After seeing them today, I can see why! These are some big kids! They're really jazzy, too. And how come they ran through the other team's warm-ups when they first came out on the court? Poor kids on the other team didn't know what to do. Adidas show offs is what they should be called! I was hoping they would lose, but they didn't.

I did, however, have a long talk with Brandon. I told him that he's going to have to learn to channel his emotions. I told him that people are learning that they can get in his head and that he has to cry on the inside. In other words, NEVER LET THEM SEE YOU SWEAT.

***

On our way back to Florida, Efrem had a long talk with Coach Don. He told Don that if they didn't recruit and get some stronger players, that Brandon would not be playing in the Memphis Nationals next year. Don assured Efrem that more talent was on the horizon. We shall see. For now, the AAU season is officially over!

Junior High Year Two

(2004-2005 School year)

Brandon just informed me that he made the team again this year (gee, what a surprise). His coach from last year, Ms. Patrick, will be sitting on the throne again. Oh boy!

At the thought of Ms. Patrick, I must laugh. She has to be the most unconventional teacher I've ever met. She takes the boys to get haircuts, gives them cough medicine, and has Brandon coaching the team. I love her, but you have to know that you're in trouble when the coach pulls Brandon off the floor and asks him what they should do next!

This year, I expect much of the same. I'm looking forward to it, but I'm also looking forward to the matchup between Brandon and Kenny (from his rec league days) again. Last year, Kenny looked like he wanted no part of Brandon. I suspect that this year, he doesn't either.

Who Threw It!

We're in semi-finals, and the unexpected has happened. Someone threw a bottle at Brandon. I think this school thought they were going to run through Brandon's team simply because they were a team from the suburbs. They didn't count on one thing: Brandon's 30+ points! That being said, the fans got frustrated, and someone threw a bottle onto the court at Brandon. Needless to say, it was on like a skillet of fried chicken! Efrem stood up in the

24

stands, looked around, and demanded to know who threw it! The gym got silent as he paraded up and down the bleachers demanding to know WHO THREW IT! People have a tendency to look at me like they feel sorry for me during these times. I really think they think I live with a tyrant at the house. Ha! Anyways, the game was halted and school officials called the cops. About fifteen minutes passed when four cops showed up. Since the gym had gotten calm (Efrem included) the cops allowed the officials to resume the game and the rest of the minute and nineteen seconds were played. Can someone say this is ONLY a junior high school game? I mean, really, is it that serious?

Afterwards, the principal instructed all players and cheerleaders to stay put until they were escorted by the police. The players and the cheerleaders sat on the bleachers while everyone from the opposing school filed out of the gym. It was about 9 pm and Efrem had to be at work around 1 am. Efrem being Efrem informed the principal that he did not teach his son to be soft and that he didn't have time to wait on a police escort because he had to go to work. He also told the man that they would be leaving the same way they came, through the front door. To top it off, he looked at Brandon and Brandon's best friend and fellow teammate, Byron, and told them they better be ready to fight if necessary. The cheerleaders sat sadly by and moaned, "Brandon, please don't go." Efrem politely escorted the boys out the gym as if he didn't have a care in the world. The school officials sat stunned, the cheerleaders looked as if they were about to cry and the rest of the remaining crowd from the opposite team actually looked afraid!

Another day at the office…er, I mean gym!

Season Over
We lost the Junior High Championship, and of course, we all sang a familiar song, "THEY CHEATED!" No, really, I really do believe they did…this time…REALLY!

Side Note: Somewhere down the road Brandon picked-up a girlfriend! A GIRLFRIEND! Imagine my shock when I gave this little girl a ride home and both of them piled in the back seat of my car and held hands! I truly had an "I don't know what to do," mama moment. I wanted to tell somebody to get their behind in the front seat, but all I did was crank up the car like Morgan Freeman in *Driving Miss Daisy. At least she's cute!*

The Jammers Year Five

(Summer 2005)

The year flew by so quickly. And here we are again in the heat of AAU season. Today, we're going to play the world famous Dream Team. According to everyone in Florida, they can't be beat. I say they can. I met the coach at the registration table, and he seemed like a nice enough guy.

Somewhere along the line, I think I've become a coward. Me, a coward! I can't bear to watch games anymore. I stay in the hallways and talk to the concession people or the security people and write journal entries, which is what I'm doing now. As kids come and go from the gym where we're playing the Dream Team, I ask the score. So far so good. We're hanging with them.

Bad news…just when it seemed we had the Dream Team on their backs, somebody poked Brandon in the eye. It's bad because he can't continue to play. Efrem is fired up about it. He swears the coach instructed one of the kids to give Brandon the dagger. I told him he's being ridiculous, but he doesn't want to hear it. Brandon has scratched his eyeball and has been prescribed drops by one of the parents (a doctor). Oh, how I wanted to beat The Dream Team!!! But it just wasn't meant to be. Good thing is there's always the next time.

Enemies to Friends – Friends to Enemies
Somewhere along the line, we became friends with the Dream Team's coach. When and where did this happen? I can't tell you. All I know is that Efrem has forgiven him for the phantom sin of instructing one of his kids to poke Brandon in the eye. It's funny … it's really funny to me. Ha! Anyway, T.J., the Dream Team's coach, wants Brandon to go to nationals with them. His team has consistently gone to the elite 8 and final 4 in each of the preceding tournaments. After much discussion we decided to let Brandon go.

***

Today we discussed Brandon going to the nationals with Don and nothing could have prepared us for what followed. Don, told us that if Brandon doesn't go with the Jammers, he's not going to go at all. Huh? Apparently, Brandon participated in a game that helped the Jammers qualify for the nationals. Once a kid participates in a qualifier, he's "stuck" to that team unless the team decides not to go. I feel like an idiot because I didn't read the rules…lesson learned. This will never happen again! EVER! In the future, before I play the game, I will know the rules of engagement.

***

Over the past few days, this Dream Team thing has turned into a war! The AAU officials have found a loophole to let Brandon play with the Dream Team and still let the Jammers go to the nationals. All the Jammer coach had to do was release Brandon. Surprise...Don said no! The parents took a vote, and they all said no also! The Jammer parents have turned on us—even the people we thought were our friends. As much as Brandon wants to play, Efrem and I have decided that we won't be buffaloed into making Brandon play with the Jammers. We've remained loyal for years despite the fact that we knew Brandon needed to play with older kids. Despite it all, we really don't want to stop playing with the Jammers; we just want to play with the Dream Team in the nationals. By doing so Brandon will have a chance to at least get to the elite 8 and get nationally ranked. Well, we're at a standoff, and nobody's budging.

The Aftermath

It's been a month since the nationals, and we all sat at home during that week depressed. It's not over; however, the plot thickens. Apparently, Brandon can't participate in any AAU games with another team this summer. This really sucks. There's still a month or so left in the season, and he's being treated like he has the plague. Who would have thought AAU sports would be like this? It's almost like other people own your kid. I know rules are rules, but given the fact that we've stayed so long, and Brandon has given this team a 100% every time he stepped on the court, you would think the coach could have given him the one thing he's asked in return. This has taught us all a lesson. Know the rules, and know that in the end, people only care about what benefits them. Unfortunately, Brandon has learned a very valuable lesson at a very young age…people care more about him as a player than him as a person.

The Eagles Year One

(July 2005)

Fly Like an Eagle

Good news! Efrem has a friend, Johnny, who has a 16-year-old team called the Hollywood Eagles. Johnny told Efrem to bring Brandon over to their practice gym, and he will let him play for the rest of the season. I'm really excited but nervous at the same time. Brandon is a baby, and these kids are 16. I know he's good, but I'm not sure about this.

Let the Games Begin

Today was Brandon's first game with the Eagles. I'm surprised at how well he has adjusted. For one thing, he has never not been a starting player since playing AAU Basketball. I asked him how he felt about it, and he said he didn't mind because he was learning a lot. He does, however, get a lot of playing time. It's funny to see him look back at Johnny every time Johnny yells or substitutes. He looks as if he's saying, "Do I need to leave? Did I do something wrong?" The Eagle parents are proud of him as well as all of the players. Several of the players have taken Brandon under their wing and are treating him like a little brother. What's amazing is that even though they can play in AAU tournaments, they will have to forfeit any trophies they win since Brandon is ineligible. The team all took a vote and they all said they didn't care … just let Brandon play! I think they rock!!!

31

***

There are only a few games left before the new school year starts. I'm glad Brandon can play for the rest of the summer, and I feel like he's where he needs to be. In the end, you know what they say, "Everything happens for a reason."

Pine Crest Year One

(2005 – 2006 School Year)

We got a call from a coach by the name of David Beckerman today. A few weeks ago, we talked to one of his assistants and expressed interest in the school. We didn't know that he'd taken us seriously (since we weren't really serious about it ourselves!), but he invited us to visit Pine Crest, which is one of the top academic schools in the country. I've always heard a lot about this school, but because of the tuition (rumored to be around $18,000), I never thought it was possible. Efrem will go visit tomorrow and tell me what he thinks. Brandon will be starting the eighth grade, and since this school goes from Pre-K to the twelfth grade, I'm hoping this will be the last school decision we'll have to make. I'm curious to find out what tomorrow brings.

***

Well, Efrem visited the school today, and boy, did he sound impressed. He said the school looks more like a college campus than that of a high school. Brandon and I have an appointment to go next week. I'm excited. Although Pine Crest is not known for sports, Efrem and I have decided that sports will take care of itself. AAU basketball will propel him where he needs to go. I think Brandon is brilliant, therefore he has to be challenged at school as well as on the court. At his present school, he finishes his homework in 30 minutes, and he's outside. He's making straight A's and he's in honors classes, but

33

it doesn't seem like he's being challenged academically. Hmmm, maybe Pine Crest will be the answer.

***

Today, Brandon and I went to Pine Crest. It's simply awesome. Efrem was right; the campus does look like that of a college. Brandon had to take a test to get in, and the admissions lady was impressed. She said he did exceptionally well! Yaay! The coach, who I don't know if I like, informed me that although Brandon may get straight A's at his present school, he probably won't get them at Pine Crest. What kind of caca is that??? After taking a moment to recover from his obvious lack of faith in Brandon's academic talent, I looked him straight in the eye and informed him that I could assure him that Brandon would get straight A's at Pine Crest. Afterwards, in the car, I begged Brandon to not let me end up with egg on my face! I was like, "Boy, you better prove me right." Ha! Brandon has expressed his disinterest in going to Pine Crest all day, but the way Efrem and I see it, he's going to get an $18,000-a-year education. Plus, instead of playing six games per year at his present school, he'll be playing 22 games a year at Pine Crest. He'll be playing varsity (assuming he's going to make the team) basketball as an eighth grader!

***

It's been a week since visiting Pine Crest. The coach called me to discuss our decision. He keeps telling me how great the academics are compared to Brandon's present school (we live in one of the top school districts in South Florida). I finally had to tell him that I work at a hospital with plenty of brain surgeons and guess what? THEY DIDN'T ALL GO TO PINE CREST! We have, however, come to a decision. Brandon will attend Pine Crest. He will get a partial scholarship because of our salaries. We can't think of a better way to spend our money so we're onboard. I'm excited and I'm really looking forward to the first of the school year. Go panthers!

Practice, School, Practice
It seems all Brandon does is go to practice and study. I knew the curriculum was intense at Pine Crest, but I had no idea it was this crazy. Brandon's day starts around 6am and doesn't end until midnight. Last night as Brandon sat at the kitchen table studying, I heard him mumble, "I see why they don't have any athletes at this school!" He's struggling in Spanish, too. For the most part, the kids who have been at the school for many grade levels are all building on what they've learned previously. Brandon has to come in and catch up. He confided in me and told me that he may not get an A in Spanish and that he's more worried about Efrem's reaction rather than getting his first B or maybe even a C. I talked to Efrem about it, and his response was this, "Brandon has shown me that he's capable of earning straight A's. I expect nothing less. When we start accepting B's, we'll start accepting C's and then D's." So much for me trying to circumvent the process. There is a light at the end of the tunnel, however. I spoke with his Spanish teacher and she will tutor him after school.

On another note, instead of taking physical education, he can go to study hall (this should help cut down some of the late nights). Apparently, if you play a sport at Pine Crest, you can elect to take study hall instead of physical education. Another good thing is that if you maintain a certain GPA, you get a free period. I'm hoping these periods without classes will help Brandon with accomplishing his academic workload.

At Last

Game day is here at last. All of the boys must dress up before each game. They wear slacks, a shirt, and tie, and get this ... a sweater! Brandon's coach is from Connecticut. This is Florida! It's 89-degrees outside! Coach B wants the kids to look preppy and sophisticated. Let's just hope nobody passes out from a heat stroke. That definitely wouldn't be sophisticated! Ha! Sweaters aside, I can't wait for tonight! All of the AAU games, etc. has led to this moment: high school. Brandon is one of the few kids playing on a varsity team as an eighth grader in south Florida, and I'm curious to see how he measures up. Playing with the older kids on the Eagles team had to have been a positive thing. I'm hoping the fruits of Brandon's labor are ripe tonight.

***

We came, we played, and we conquered. Brandon more than held his own at the high school level. He scored over 20 points and led his team to a victory! I can't wait to see what the year brings!!!

36

Spirit Schmirit

Where's the love? Where's the love? At any given game, there are only a handful of fans. My impression of high school basketball was different from this! I pictured school spirit coming out of the concrete of the gym, and boy, was I wrong. The cheerleaders (from what I'm told) were told by the Athletic Director that if they didn't cheer at the games, they couldn't compete in their own cheerleading competitions. So needless to say, they're at the games by default. De-fault of the Athletic Director (ha)! To make matters worse, I haven't heard them utter a cheer yet! Huh? Seriously, not even a "GO TEAM GO!" Humph! If it weren't for the hip-hop dancers, about 10 girls, none of which are African American, the place would be dead during halftime and the time outs. Now, I don't mean to talk bad about the hip-hop dancers, but suffice it to say that they won't be dancing for MC Hammer (or whoever is in style these days) any time soon! They do, however, try and that's more than I can say about the cheerleaders.

Rivalry Isn't Dead

Last week, we played two teams with former Jammer players. Brandon was hyped. He was ready to play them, and play them he did. We won both matches! The first game was against a school called North Broward Prep. They scheduled their homecoming against us because they figured it would be a happy ending (as it has been in the past). Unfortunately for them, it turned out bad! They had a Pine Crest prop outside that they had planned on burning after their "victory" against us. Somewhere around the third quarter, they dismantled everything, tucked their tails between their legs, and sat in stunned silence as they watched Brandon put on a show. The coach from the Jammers, Don, had a son playing on the second team we annihilated (Highlands Christian). I feel kinda bad since the guy tried to say hello, and all we did was ignore him. I know it's time to let this thing go, but how do you let something go when you're still fired up? Hmmmm.

***

Tonight we played Pine Crest's rivalry, Westminster, and lost. They have this kid on their team who's as thin as a rail. He plays pretty well, but here's the catch: Blow on him, and he's at the free throw line (and he doesn't miss either). I've never seen anything like it. You can't even look like you want to touch this kid because if you do, the refs are blowing the whistle. I don't want to say they cheated, but …

***

Yesterday, we played American Heritage. Their fans were horrible! Let me repeat, HORRIBLE. First of all, they had a DJ in their tiny little gym. Second, the DJ's speakers were set right behind the visiting team's bench - OUR bench - which made it impossible for us to hear our coach. Finally, they taunted the players on the opposite team - OUR team - the entire time the game was being played. Those bad behind kids stood on the sidelines with signs that said, "Knight, Knight! It's your bed time!" I guess since Brandon is an eighth grader, they feel he's a baby and should probably be home getting some rest. Too bad the baby ripped their hearts out and scored 18 points on them. Guess it was a "Good Knight," and THEY should probably be the ones going to bed!

Enemies in the Camp

Brandon has been in the newspaper a lot, and there's been a little envy (in my opinion) from his teammates. The seniors and juniors refuse to give him the ball. The father of one of the senior players came to me and said, "Brandon's trying to do it all. He should pass the ball to my son more often." There's only one problem, his son can't shoot! Here we go again. Good thing we're used to it. AAU parents have taught us very well. The beat truly goes on.

Westminster on the Ropes

We played Westminster tonight, a team Pine Crest has not won against in more than 20 years. Students, teachers, parents, and fans are coming out more and more to support their Pine Crest team; I guess everyone loves a winner and guess what? Tonight, we won!!! Brandon was on the free throw line with three seconds left. We were down by one, and Brandon hit both free throws. When the whistle blew, the crowd rushed the floor! I mean, about 500 kids rushed onto the floor! I will remember this night forever because we took out Westminster when nobody thought we would. What a night! Or should I say, WHAT A KNIGHT!!!

What a Year!

(March 2006)

Tonight, we played our regional finals and lost. To make things worse, we lost to Westminster. Oh, the agony of defeat. The pain, the pain! And true to their nature, the seniors refused to pass the ball to Brandon during the game. I'm not saying that Brandon was our only hope to beat Westminster, but he was our best hope. I'm so happy that we don't have to face this situation next year. The seniors will be gone. One is leaving for college on a baseball scholarship, and the other one is going on a football scholarship.

That's amazing to me. Basketball wasn't even their top sport priority, but they still gave their teammate grief during the games. You see, if a senior didn't hit the winning shot, then nobody was going to do it—especially not an eighth grader. It's the same story everywhere. Brandon plays well, and in one way or the other, he's going to be penalized for it either by not being allowed to play with the team of his choice, sitting the bench for scoring too many points, or having his own teammates harboring resentment. It bothers me, but what can I do? This has become his world, and thus, it has become ours. All things considered, it's been great. What a year!

P.S. I haven't seen Brandon cry all season. He took my advice. NEVER LET THEM SEE YOU SWEAT!

P.P.S. Brandon earned straight A's this year!! I couldn't wait to rub it into Coach Beckerman's face! He laughed and said, "I know, I know." I've truly grown to love Coach B. He's an exceptional human being, and he truly loves the kids on his team. Coach B is a millionaire; seriously. He donates his salary to the school. That being said, everyone knows that Coach B's coaching at Pine Crest is a labor of love. He always says, "All I care about are the kids," and I believe him. He's one of the few coaches that want absolutely nothing from the kids he coaches but what's best for them.

Eagles Year Two

(Summer 2006)

It's AAU time, and Johnny has plans on playing in Memphis next week with his Hollywood Eagles. According to him, it's supposed to be a great tournament, but there's just one catch. Johnny hasn't secured transportation for the team. Johnny's funny. He has a big heart and big plans, but little funding. But, despite the lack of funding, there's one good thing to be said about the team: they have a nice home uniform! Okay, I don't mean to crack jokes on the uniform situation (yes, I do), but there's only ONE. No away uniform, just a powder-blue home uniform with the Hollywood Eagles written on the front and of course, the player's number on the back. What's funnier is Johnny's obsession over his uniforms. There is NO taking his uniforms home … under no circumstances! Even Ray (the team's star) can't take a uniform home. If the kids need to strip down to bare bottoms and go home naked to give Johnny his uniforms back after a game, then so be it.

Drive Like an Eagle
Efrem just asked me if I plan on going with him and the team to a tournament in Memphis. My answer? No, double no, uh, make that a triple no! Apparently Johnny's transportation woes have been resolved. Johnny has a passenger van, and he's planning on driving it to Memphis. What? I can't even imagine

42

sitting in a 12-passenger van with eight kids funking up the joint! You know there's bound to be foot funk, butt funk, underarm funk, need I continue? Ugggh! Efrem comes back at my "no" by saying I'm not supporting the team (just a ploy to get me to suffer with him). My answer? "If this is what's required to support the team, they will be unsupported!" As for me, I'll be sitting by our pool relaxing with my girlfriends this weekend. See ya next week, Efrem and Brandon!

***

The Memphis trip was fun ... according to Efrem. Brandon, however, wants to know why did all the other teams arrive by plane, and they were the only one's pulling up in a van? I can't help but laugh because I'm sure he's not the only kid with that thought. Johnny simply laughs. He's a man with a plan, but no money in his hand. WE HAVE TO FIND SOME SPONSORS! Next week, they'll be headed to Houston, and this time they'll take a bus. Efrem wants to know if I'll be riding on the bus. Nope, no, no way, ain't gonna happen. Same funk rules apply. There's just more room for the funk to circulate in a bus versus a van!

Lodge Like an Eagle
Efrem just called me from Houston. They're in a hotel that he claims has roach eggs on the bed and mold around the refrigerator. He says he went to the local store and got some Lysol. I don't think that'll sanitize the roach motel, but I don't want to discourage him. He sounded pretty torn up about it as it was. After hanging

43

up from him, I have only one thing to say: "Boy, am I glad I elected to stay home and sit by the pool with my buddies." I would have been fired up if I were in Houston. I definitely would have demanded we find a more inhabitable hotel. WE HAVE TO FIND SOME SPONSORS! Didn't I say that at least ten times already?

***

The fellas are back from Houston, and they look beat down. A 20-hour bus ride will do that to you. I cooked them a fancy meal, and they thanked me by looking grateful. Ha! Next week, we'll be in Orlando. I'll go to that trip since we'll be getting our own hotel and driving our car. In the meantime, all is at peace in the Knight house.

One Man's Junk
Throughout Brandon's playing career, we've had the privilege of playing in Orlando on several occasions. Today was no different. Brandon is 14 and playing with 17-year-old kids. He's on the starting lineup these days, and he looks like a real floor general. I love the fact that Johnny has the utmost confidence in his abilities. Everyone is telling me how well he played in Houston. I'm a little sorry I didn't go (well, not really).

***

Today, Brandon played exceptionally well but unfortunately, we came in second. The Eagles parents (which are voted the worst on the internet) went berserk!

44

The refs really did cheat this time. For some reason, they don't care for Johnny. Some say it's because his teams always win, and some say it's because he's a touch arrogant. In any event, the kids are not responsible for any of it. It's a shame that the adult human factor filters into kid's basketball. To make matters worse, Johnny (along with some of the kids) threw the second place trophies in the trash ... at the gym! I know our reputation has gone straight down the tube over this stunt. Several of the other area coaches have already called me this afternoon in disbelief. I'm just glad we're out of here tomorrow. I kinda miss our Jammer days. Although I heard a few slick comments from those parents, they did, on the surface, remain friendly. These Eagle parents are straight up off the chain this year! They have started to complain about a 14-year-old kid starting in front of their kids to our face, and trust me, they are not friendly. During one of our earlier games this year, one of the parents got on the court and threatened the ref! Efrem might talk trash to them, but he's never threatened anyone. To put it bluntly, this sucks! Something's got to give. What's a basketball mom to do?

Win a Few, Win a Few

The summer is almost over. We won almost everything we entered. We didn't go to the AAU Nationals, but we did do a lot of other tournaments. There were scrapes along the way, and there was some peace (a rare occurrence). I'm just glad this summer is coming to an end. Efrem and I are looking for alternatives. We have to go to a team that has funding. If Brandon is going to be ranked and stay on the basketball radar of the powers that be, he's going to have to play on the big stage. Unfortunately, Johnny can't seem to land the funding. Oh well. We have a whole year to think about it. T.J. has asked us to let Brandon play with the Dream Team several times. There's just one problem with that. T.J. is in Orlando, and we're here in Ft Lauderdale. Practice is impossible, and we just don't think it's a good fit because of the logistics. Again, we have another year to think this through. Help!

Pine Crest Year Two

(2006 – 2007 School Year)

It's been a while since my last entry. The beginning of school launched pretty much like it did last year: lots of home work and plenty of practice. Today was our first game, and everyone was pretty excited. I must say that the crowd has picked up tremendously compared to last year. The cheerleaders, however, are still pretty much comatose. Well, I take that back. To their credit, I think they said "Go PC" a couple of times. I hope I'm wrong, but I could have sworn I saw one of them filing a fingernail and another one yawning.

Is He Serious?

Let me just start off by saying I love Coach Beckerman. Now that that's been said, let me say this: Coach Beckerman is a mother hen. Seriously, he reminds me of somebody's granny! Tonight, Brandon cut his lip. Not a bad cut, but it was a cut nonetheless. I can't even recall how many times Brandon's lip has been cut or he's been poked in the eye. As parents, we're used to it. No biggie. To Coach Beckerman, it's catastrophic. After tonight's game, he walked up to us and told us Brandon needed to go to the ER and asked if we needed recommendations for a plastic surgeon. What??? IT'S A CUT LIP! Is he serious??? We told him we've seen worse, but he didn't want to hear it. After much discussion and debate, Efrem finally goes, "Look, man, I'm not taking Brandon to the ER for a cut lip. Stop being a mother hen." Coach

47

Beckerman turned red and walked away. I guess he was serious after all!

American Heritage Part 1
Tonight, we played American Heritage. They have three nationally ranked players on their team, and one of them is Kenny Boynton (not the Kenny from rec league days). Kenny is one of my favorite kids. He's really a great kid and a great basketball player. For quite some time, everyone has been comparing Kenny and Brandon. The great debate is who is better: Kenny or Brandon. There's plenty of hype around this game. I'm nervous!

***

Well, tonight was the Heritage/Pine Crest pow wow! We won … we won … we won!!! I'm getting to be a nervous wreck these days. I can't stay in the gym during the games. I especially couldn't sit still for this one. The gym was packed! It seems people were pouring in from the rafters. When it was all said and done, Pine Crest emerged victorious. Everyone said we couldn't do it, but we did. Brandon had 28 points, and once again, he rocked!

***

It's been a couple of months since we played American Heritage. Tonight, we'll face them for the second time this season. The newspapers are hyping the event up, and everyone is calling us for tickets. Who do they think we are, Ticketmaster? So far, we've purchased tickets totaling a little more than $200. Everyone claims they will pay us back (sure they will). For some reason, people think we're rich. They act like Brandon is in the NBA or something. Newsflash: Efrem and I work every day! So I say to them, "No money, no ticket." Efrem tells me not to "be like that." Like what? I want our money!

***

We won...we won...we won!!! Once again, lowly Pine Crest beat American Heritage! These games get more nerve-wracking by the minute. I seriously can't stand to be in the gym. The energy is tangible, and yes, Efrem is still yelling at the refs. Ha! After the game, Brandon was on cloud nine, and the kids at the school came out to support the team in droves. Rarely does Brandon show any overt emotions or brag about himself. I love that about him. He's very humble, and I'm not just saying that because I'm his mom. He just isn't full of himself. I've waited a long time to see Brandon play in such a big setting, and it was awesome. I just hope it was as awesome for him as it was for me. Tonight, I will go to sleep with a smile on my face.

***

The last two times we played American Heritage, we won. Before we can advance to the regional finals, we must beat them again. Tension is high and the game is expected to be sold out. Pine Crest is going to show the game outside on a projection screen for the people who won't be able to get inside the gym. Once again, the newspapers are hyping the game, and once again, I am a train wreck.

***

Last week, we beat American Heritage once again!!! They have some of the greatest players in the country on their team (many nationally ranked). The only nationally ranked person on Pine Crest's team is Brandon. Nobody can figure out how we win. But the fact is, we do win! Tonight, we played a team called LaSalle to determine if we would go to the state championships. Tonight, we won!!! How exciting is it for Pine Crest to be going to their first state championship, ever? School spirit drips from the sky. Pine Crest rocks!

Going to the "Ship"
Due to work commitments, Efrem and I didn't attend the semi-finals today. I monitored the score on my computer from work, and Efrem received updates from friends attending the game. We lost the championship. I really want to cry. Not much to say but … there's always next year.

Breakdown Year One

(Summer 2007)

Summer is among us and so is another AAU season.
Johnny came to Efrem today with a proposal. There's a
team called Breakdown in South Florida. They are one
of the premier teams and have wanted Brandon to play
for them for quite some time. They offered Johnny a job
as an assistant coach, and Johnny presented Efrem with
the idea today. Efrem was a little shaky on the idea since
he thinks (1) the owners (all brothers) are a bunch of
immature kids, and (2) they wear pink uniforms. Johnny
somehow convinced Efrem to go along with the idea,
and so it will be.

Let The Games Begin
Today was the first Breakdown game. Madness and
mayhem prevailed … seriously! The brothers all sit on
the first bleacher to taunt (and I do mean taunt) the
players from the other teams. They call them by name,
and they scream when the kids miss shots. My personal
favorite is when they yell, "Hot potato, you don't want
it," each time a poor kid passes the ball. The parents
from the other teams were heated, and rightfully so. I
know I'd be heated if a bench load of grown men taunted
Brandon during a game! The kids get rattled and start to
resemble a bunch of bumbling idiots. This, of course,
only provides more entertainment for the brothers. The
brothers do, however, have funding, and I mean plenty
of it. The kids stay in nice hotels, and they travel by
airplane. Something tells me that playing with

Breakdown is going to be a wild ride. And I can say this much, they have a heck of a squad. Some of the top kids in the country play for Breakdown. Kenny Boynton and Brandon will be playing side-by-side. Kenny is a warrior. The "Who's better...Kenny or Brandon?" debate has started up again. Thankfully so far, both parents on both sides of the debate have remained removed.

Qualifying at Disney
Today, we won the 16-and-up tournament, which is a Disney AAU Tournament. At any given tournament, there are over 100 teams from all over the country playing. We've been winning a lot lately. Everyone has something slick to say about the pink and black uniforms, but what can you do? Not my team, not my uniform. The brothers seem to think the uniforms are an intimidation factor. They say that when teams see the fellas in pink, they think they're soft, and then they get a one-two punch. Huh? Again, huh? Reminds me of something my mama used to say, "Your definition of normal is somebody else's strange." Ok, enough about the uniforms; let me move on to the awards ceremony. The awards ceremony takes the cake at Disney. We've been playing at Disney for years, and it just floors me when they pass out the medals at the end of the tournament. How come they just give a handful of medals to the coach and leave?? No standing on platforms, no music being played, no announcements, nothing! And this is an upstanding place, too! There are about six gyms all under one roof. Pictures of various athletes (all wearing milk mustaches) hang from the

ceiling (hence the gym's name: The Milk House). Plus, a huge restaurant, soccer field, and baseball field are all on the complex. Get the picture? This is not the elementary school's gym down the road. This is Disney! So I say all that to say this, WHY CAN'T THEY HAVE A CEREMONY??? You know, make the kids feel special? Maybe I should write somebody …

I Wanna Go Home!
We have been on the road this summer more than we've been home. Every weekend it seems we are packing clothes and running off to an airport after work on a Friday evening. How I long to relax for a weekend in my own bed. Oh, the sacrifices we make for our children! Efrem and I could probably stay home, but Brandon is 15. We just feel better travelling with him to make sure he doesn't bow to peer pressure. He's playing with older kids, and the brothers aren't big on supervision, so Efrem and I figured we better exercise due diligence. We've missed a couple of trips, but Johnny was there. Johnny is 40-ish, and he's old school just like Efrem. He does room checks. Brandon is pretty levelheaded and, from what we can tell, not a follower. But you never know. Always assume your teenager is the enemy until he/she is no longer a teenager…Ha!

Carolina Blues
We're in North Carolina at the Bob Gibbons Tournament, and we got to play both in Duke's gym and in North Carolina's gym. Duke's gym sure looks different than I pictured. It's small and very intimate. It's kind of retro. My guess is that it will never be renovated

because tradition definitely prevails here. As for North Carolina's gym, it's huge. It's exactly what one would picture a college gym to look like. All of this is very exciting. For the first time, I'm actually picturing Brandon playing college basketball in a college gym. I sure hope he plays somewhere with a lot of tradition and fans. I love tradition. It's funny that until now, I really haven't given much thought to Brandon playing for a large college. Sure there's letters in the mail from different colleges, but I just never really thought about him playing in front of thousands of fans and on TV. I know that it's going to happen for him (God willing). He's focused and very talented. He was just ranked number one among his peers, so if that's any indication, he's off to great things on the court. I just pray he stays humble. There's nothing worse than a kid acting like he's an all star and hasn't even played one game in the NBA. I have had the displeasure of meeting several of these kids, and they are no fun. One even had the audacity to get offended because Efrem said he didn't know who he was! He looked at Efrem and said, "You mean you don't know who I am? You haven't seen me playing on Sun TV?" (which is a local Florida Channel) In true Efrem fashion, Efrem looked at the kid and said, "Son, I never heard of you." To make matters worse, Efrem didn't crack a smile.

Vegas, Vegas, Vegas
Vegas is one of the largest tournaments of the summer, and we made it to the championship! Everyone is saying Breakdown has the toughest backcourt in the country with Brandon and Kenny. Too bad we didn't prove

54

everyone right. At the buzzer, a kid by the name of Brandon Jennings (now with the Milwaukee Bucks) came down and hit a three. That hurt! What goes on in Vegas doesn't always stay in Vegas. In this case, it's coming back home to Florida.

Next...
It's been a couple of days since the Vegas blow. The team immediately flew from Vegas to Disney for the Nationals. How exciting that we are now National Champions! That's right, we had to go through a lot of tough teams that are loaded with the top players in the country to get the gold, but we did it! WE ARE NATIONAL CHAMPIONS! It's funny that Brandon has played WITH three kids from American Heritage this summer and will play AGAINST them again when school starts. How weird is that?

Free at Last
The summer is over and rest is on the horizon. It was a great summer. We won, we won, we won!!!

Pine Crest Year Three

(2007-2008 School Year)

It was a great summer, but it's back to hard work for Brandon. He's taking a load of honors and advanced placement classes these days. He seems to have basketball and school all under wraps. He has become the master of time management. I guess Brandon has taken his dad's warning seriously: as soon as his grades, slip basketball will be over!

To Whom Much Is Given...
The Bible says, "To whom much is given, much is required." I definitely think that's the case with Brandon. Last night, I woke up to take a potty break and saw a light on in the kitchen. I followed the light into the kitchen and peeped around the corner. At the table sat Brandon at 2:30 in the morning studying. Four hours later, I had to wake him to get ready for school. I worry about him. I worry that the combination of basketball and the rigorous academics at Pine Crest are too much. He says he's fine. He loves Pine Crest, therefore placing him in another school isn't the solution. Having a kid that's a perfectionist is hard. Having a kid that's gifted in academics and athletics is even harder. Finding a healthy balance between it all is next to impossible. What's a mother to do?

A Little Rain Must Fall

(Although I will share what happened during this period, I won't go into great detail. I believe this story is Brandon's to share, and in his own time, he will).

A few weeks ago, Brandon asked me to make an appointment with his doctor. He said his arm felt "funny." I took him to the doctor, and his physician ordered an MRI. Today, I got the results. It seems there's a cyst on his spine. The doctor seemed devastated, Efrem and I are devastated. This is something that's rare, and after looking on the internet, it seems dire. The school has stopped Brandon from practicing. Efrem and I picked him up from school and had to explain to him the seriousness of the situation. He may not be able to play basketball ... ever again. He cried, I cried, Efrem cried, and we prayed.

***

After finding out the doctor's report from yesterday, I haven't been able to eat or sleep. Today, Brandon has to have another MRI, and then we're going to see a neurosurgeon. I know that the sun doesn't shine every day, and into everyone's life a little rain must fall. This is a downpour, and for right now, I feel as though I'm drowning. Thank God for my friend Avis. I called her crying, and she told me keep praying because in the end, God has the final say. Not the doctors, not what I read on the internet, only God. Avis is a miracle. She received an artificial heart valve when she was a kid (around three or four years old). The doctors gave her a 20% chance of survival, and she made it. They said she wouldn't live past her teen years, and she did. They also said she would never have children or lead a normal life, but she did. Thank you, Avis. I love you!

***

The MRI took four hours. Afterwards, we went to get something to eat, and then we headed to the neurosurgeon. I used to work with one of the medical assistants in the neurosurgeon's office. Last year, she lost her 16-year-old daughter to brain cancer. After seeing her, I put everything into perspective. Forget about basketball! Forget about any deficits neurologically. Just let my child live.

Brandon, on the other hand, had a different experience (which is his story to tell), but suffice it to say he experienced a miracle while sitting in the waiting room. Afterwards, he had the most peaceful look on his face. His demeanor became calm, a calm that was almost tangible. When I asked him if he was nervous, he simply said, "For what? I'm going to be just fine." True to his prediction, he is fine, at least for now. The neurosurgeon said the cyst was small and spinal fluid was flowing around it. He was cleared to play basketball for the rest of the season. In six months, he will have another MRI to see where he stands.

Heritage Again
The venue has been changed for our game against American Heritage. It seems the school gyms are too

small to accommodate the crowd. The game has been moved to a local public gym. As usual, everyone is calling for tickets. You would think this is the Final Four or the NBA Playoffs!

***

True to my cowardly self, I didn't go to the game! I know, I know, this is history! I just can't stand it!! It's like being bound by a tension rope or something. I used to call Efrem for updates, but he no longer answers his phone. Umph! Thank God for Kenny Boynton's mom. She's the text queen! She sends me regular updates via text. Even though we find ourselves on opposite sides of the fence, we've remained friends. We cheer for each other's kids, and when people come to me about this stupid "Who's Better: Kenny or Brandon?" crap, I let them have it! Why can't people just celebrate two great basketball players? Why must there always be a comparison. I hate it. I simply hate it. Well, once again, we won. Congrats to American Heritage for giving us a run for our money.

In the 'Ship Once Again
It's been an intense, tough, and incredibly hard year. But we've managed to earn our way to another state appearance. This year, our team is strong, and I really, really think we can do it. Efrem and I aren't missing anything this year. We are both here and can't wait for the tournament to begin.

***

We're one step closer to winning a state championship! We advanced to the championship today. We had a lot of fans in the audience. T.J. and Johnny will be here tomorrow for the championship games. It's really funny how relationships develop. Who would have ever thought T.J. would become a close family friend after Efrem swore he instructed one of his players to poke Brandon in the eye? It seems like forever since we first played the infamous Dream Team. Even though Brandon plays with Breakdown, T.J. has always supported Brandon and has been to all of his games (when we play in Orlando). The state championship is about 45 minutes from Orlando, so of course, T.J. will be there. Along the way, we've made friends and, of course, some enemies. I'm just thankful that the friends we made are good ones!

***

We are officially State Champions! Yes!!! The game was nip and tuck in the beginning. To make matters worse, there was a truly obnoxious fan sitting behind us. His kid played for the opposite team, and he didn't shut up. I tried to ignore him, and ignore him I did for most of the game. It wasn't until Brandon got hurt (nothing serious) that I popped a spring. How come he screamed, "GOOD! GET HIM OUT OF THERE!" Huh? What parent in their right mind rejoices when a kid is hurt?

60

Well, that's when the she-lion came out of her den. I stood up, turned around, and cussed him straight out. Let me just say this. I am a Christian woman—an upstanding and respectable citizen (for the most part). I don't make it a habit to do a lot of cussing, but this man's ignorance produced a chain reaction, a reaction that made me want to hit him up side his head with a chain! Nonetheless, this has been a happy day. We are State Champions, and it feels real good!

Breakdown Year Two

(Summer 2008)

This AAU season is grueling. We're participating in a lot of tournaments, and I'm already tired just looking at the schedule. We'll be playing in Arkansas, North Carolina, Houston, New York, and Vegas (just to name a few). To top things off, Brandon will be going to different camps: The NBA Top 100, the Nike Skills Camp, and the Boost Mobile Elite Game in Rucker's Park. Whew!

Bob Gibbons – North Carolina

Today, we played against a team in New York called the New York Gauchos. There was a man wearing a fake cow's head on his head talking about Florida basketball. He said, "If you want a running back, go to Florida. If you want a guard, come to New York." I bet he ate those words when we won! Although he gave us a lot of grief, he was actually a joy. He was funny and actually congratulated us on the win. After our game, all hell broke loose. Some of the parents were calling our kids punks because of the pink uniforms. Of course, this created problems with the parents from our team. Words were being thrown back and forward, and Efrem, never one to be passive in these situations, was front and center. To his credit, he calmed everyone down. He asked the parents from the other team why they would taunt kids. He told them that as adults, we should lift our kids up instead of putting them down, no matter the circumstances. I was shocked when everyone agreed and actually sat down to eat together. Talk about the power of words!

Real Deal on the Hill – Arkansas

We won another tournament but had to leave immediately to catch our flight. Our boys literally grabbed their trophies and ran off the court. There's only one plane leaving, and nobody wants to stay in Arkansas an extra day. Some of the kids made it, but some didn't. Me, Efrem, Brandon, and Johnny were among the fortunate few. The rest of the kids will have to stay for another day. I feel as if I'm on a roller coaster, this constant travelling, rushing, and sleeping in hotels is starting to wear me out! I can't wait for school to start. At least there's going to be a couple of months when there's no basketball! Counting the days!

Houston

There's this one kid on the team who's an instigator. If there's a pot to be stirred, he has the spoon. He's from California and, therefore, knew all of the kids (from a California team) we played in the championship today. Apparently, he went and told one of the kids on the California team that his sister was … er … let's just say…not an upstanding citizen when it comes to going out with the opposite sex. After the game, the basketball hit the fan (so to speak). Efrem and I walked out of the gym, and it was on. All of the kids and parents from Breakdown were on one side of an invisible line, and all of the parents and kids from the other team were on the other side. Of course, Efrem immediately took his designated spot — front and center. To Efrem's credit, he does try to diffuse situations when they turn bad. But if there's no peace to be made, he's not going down without a fight. By the time we arrived, things had already taken a turn for the worse. An argument started, and blows were about to be thrown. Thank God somebody had the sense to call the police. This mess is getting to be stressful. For God's sake, STOP THE MADNESS PEOPLE!

Nike Skills Camp

Very rarely does Brandon Knight get excited about anything. Let me repeat, VERY RARELY DOES BRANDON KNIGHT GET EXCITED ABOUT ANYTHING. Today was one of those rare occasions. Nike takes the top ranked kids and sends them to different cities to learn from NBA players. Brandon was selected to go to the Steve Nash Skills Camp. Today, he said he worked out with Steve himself and absolutely loved every minute of it. One of the coaches at the camp said he was the only kid taking notes. Ha! That's typical Brandon! I'm willing to bet that he's going to be practicing everything he learned once he gets home.

NBA Top 100 Camp

Kind of like the Nike Skills Camp, the NBA Top 100 Camp takes the top 100 ranked kids in the country and sends them to a designated city each year, and Brandon was selected to go. From everything we've heard, he's doing very well at the camp. Several coaches from around the country have called us to tell us that he's one of the top kids at the camp. So why did he drop from #1 in the rankings to #8? Some folks feel that the people who do the rankings feel the need to shake things up every now and then. Others feel that these people never played a game of basketball in their lives and don't know what they're talking about. I feel that it's a numbers game. Score the most points consistently and win, and you get ranked. Who knows? All I know is that Brandon is fired up. He told his dad that he worked too hard to drop so far. Hard work always pays off. In the end, things will be as they should. In other words, this too shall pass.

Prove them Wrong

If there's one thing I know it's this, YOU WILL NOT WIN THE PRATHER TOURNAMENT IN ATLANTA. Well, let me clarify. You will not win unless you flat out play. This team called the Atlanta Celtics hosts this tournament annually, and everyone knows you have to come out and club them over the heads to win. Now, I know I love to accuse the refs of cheating, but this time it's true. Ha! The coach of the Celtics is a guy named Hulio. I love Hulio, but I had to call Hulio out during one of our games today. I saw him standing across the gym and yelled, "Hulio, stop paying the refs!" He simply looked at me and cracked up laughing. I think he thinks I'm a lunatic. Needless to say, we lost the tournament in Atlanta. Brandon, however, played like I've never seen him play before. After being dropped in the rankings, he came home with his tennis shoes all marked up which read, "#8 PROVE THEM WRONG!" Prove them he did. Sometimes it's good to shake things up, it keeps one humble and hungry, two ingredients that are the key to success.

Back to the Desert

We're in Vegas and it's hot! We're from Florida, and I'm hot so that should be a witness as to how hot it is here! We've been here a week, and between the heat and all of the games, I feel like I'm about to pass out. There's only one consolation, we're taking home the brass. To win, we had to play against some of the top kids in the country, including the top ranked soon-to-be-senior John Wall. He's an awesome player, but we came, we played, and we conquered. Of course, there was an altercation. What major tournament is without one? Apparently, two sisters got into an argument over whose brother was number one. One side was from California and the other side from North Carolina (John Wall's team). Why is it always the teams from California and New York (even though New York behaved during this tournament) in the confrontations? Well, one could add Florida into the mix since we've gotten into it with both the New York and California teams. Ha! I don't know why people get into these discussions as to who's better. In the end, college and the NBA will separate the raw from the hide.

Back to Mickey

Our boys got off the plane, drove to the Disney complex, and began playing the first game in the national tournament. After playing for a week straight in Vegas (sometimes two games a day), flying across country, and then playing immediately, our boys look beat down. I don't agree with this. I just don't feel the body is made to go this hard. Brandon says he's fine. Let's hope so. I'm tired, and I haven't played a lick of basketball.

Maybe it's youth. The nationals will last for a week, and I hope the essence of youth will continue to fan their flames.

***

Once again, we're national champs!! Brandon suffered a hip contusion, and Kenny had a sprained ankle. Through it all, we won. I would probably write more, but I'm tired. Oh, Brandon got moved back up to the #1 spot. Guess he did what he said he would do, PROVE THEM WRONG!

Adidas Games

Brandon was supposed to go to France to play for the Adidas team. Efrem and I decided it's just too much. We did, however, agree to let him play at their USA games in Houston. I love their staff! They had a nutritionist come in and give the kids nutritional guidance, an exercise person who gave the kids tips on stretching and cooling down, and a guy who works with pros came in and taught the guards ball-handling drills. Everyone was impressed with Brandon's work ethic. People really look at these kids' work ethic. I overhead a staff member commenting on how some kids were just flat out lazy and how some kids worked hard. He was especially impressed with Brandon because he said Brandon was the only kid who gave 100% every time he touched a basketball. Brandon has always been taught by us to give everything 100%. Thank God he listened!

First Team

The NCAA has this program called First Team. The program consists of kids from around the country playing basketball. At the end of the summer, each kid is flown to a location (announced just before the event) where they learn things such as handling the media, etiquette, and the pitfalls of the NBA. Their slogan is, "Use Basketball, Don't Let It Use You." I love this program. Even though I know Brandon is tired, this is the one thing that Efrem and I really insist that he attends. We both feel it's important.

Boost Mobile Elite

We agreed to go to the Boost Mobile Elite game in New York, and I don't know why. I'm tired. We're all tired. To make things worse, Brandon is trippin' about his hair. School starts right after we return from New York, and he wants his braids to look fresh for school. After Vegas and Disney, his head looks like a hot mess! Brandon is fanatical about his hair. Only one person, Renea, is allowed to braid his hair. He knows I'm no braider, but has consented to let me do his hair nonetheless. I talked him into letting me put it into two strand twists, and it looks really cute. Brandon hates it.

(NOTE: There have been several pictures and magazine covers with him and that hairdo. It seemed, for a while, that he was destined to be associated with what many have called, his "dreads.")

***

The Boost Mobile Elite games are played at Rucker's Park. It's more of a fun event than anything. The kids participate in several events, and the grand finale is the game. All of the parents and kids were taken to the game via a chartered bus. Once we got there, we were greeted by a hospitality group and escorted to our seats. The park was packed! Apparently this is a huge event here in New York. Whoever organized the event did a great job. During time outs and half-time, there was plenty of entertainment. It was really funny because ESPN was there filming, and parents were turning their heads away from the camera like crazy. Many of the parents called in sick to work and absolutely, positively didn't want to be filmed ... me included! One of the parents actually (jokingly) asked the cameraman if he was trying to get him fired! Brandon played well but all-star games have never been his thing. He hates ball hogging and tries to play the game the right way. Many of the other kids simply throw the ball up every time they touch it, but Mr. Brandon refuses. Guess he won't make the highlight reel tonight!

Pine Crest Year Four

(2008-2009 School Year)

Thank God the summer is over! This has been one of the worst summers in the history of Brandon playing basketball as far as us travelling. This weekend, we're home, and I didn't leave the house. I caught up with some much needed rest. Brandon has started driving, and I gotta send a shout out to God for that! Mom's taxi is officially over. For now, I can relax without worrying about taking him to school, practice, or the movies. *Sigh*

Who's Business is it Anyway?

The season has started, and one of the most incredible things happened today. The Athletic Director called me to tell me Brandon needs to get his second MRI. Huh? Is Brandon's medical status Pine Crest's business? Pine Crest is insisting we get an MRI before Brandon is allowed to practice. We are parents who love our child. We know what he needs. We don't need the Athletic Director or anyone else telling us how to handle Brandon's medical business! Unfortunately, Brandon can't play until he's cleared. Fortunately, we already had an appointment scheduled for him. I'm heated, but I guess everyone has a job to do.

Tough Times Ahead

Today, we met one of the most incredible doctors, EVER! After talking to him, we are relieved. He has ordered another MRI, but gave us the worst-case

70

scenario. Brandon has surgery, misses a couple of months, returns to high school basketball, and later go on to the NBA. We were looking at things being a lot worse. I should probably stay off the internet. Based on everything that I've read, the end result is incontinence, neurological deficits, and paralysis. I can finally breathe. All summer long, this has been in the back of my mind.

***

The MRI results came in today. The cyst has gotten bigger, and the doctor scheduled Brandon for surgery immediately. Brandon has not suffered any neurological deficits, and they're trying to correct the problem before any deficits show up. Apparently if this cyst presses against the wrong nerves, etc., the end result could be paralysis. We have been praying about this situation continuously. Efrem asked Brandon how was his faith, and Brandon said great. As a family, this is tough, but with God's help, we will get through this.

***

On the way to the hospital this morning, Efrem and I were nervous wrecks. Neither one of us slept all night. Brandon, on the other hand, slept like a baby, both through the night and during the hour-long drive to the hospital in South Miami. Thank God the surgery was a success! The surgery lasted five hours, but as soon as Brandon got to his room, he was entertaining his friends! Kids! It's going to be a rough couple of months. Brandon has to lie on his back for a week, refrain from any weightlifting for two months and, of course, no basketball until he's completely healed. All things considered, he's blessed that this thing was contained and didn't cause him any serious damage. I thank God for His protective hedge around our family.

**

It's been a little over two weeks since the surgery, and Brandon is back to school. I drive him each morning, and someone is always waiting to carry his backpack (he can't lift anything). Pine Crest has exceptional kids! Brandon is a little grouchy because he can't play. He can't shoot a basketball or do any dribbling. As much as it must hurt him to see his teammates play while he can't, he's at every game supporting them. I'm just glad we have a healthy kid. At this point, basketball is only important to me because it's important to him.

Let the Games Begin
Brandon missed the first three months of this season, and tonight was his first game. I can't believe he scored 17 points! It was almost as if he never missed a game! Everyone cheered for him and just about every parent told me how happy they were to see him play again. During the first quarter, he took a charge, and my heart stopped until he got up off the floor. I wanted to scream, "Boy, you just had surgery on your back! Why would you stand there and let someone run into you full-speed?" Brandon's doctors said he would be as good as new, and he is. I will remain eternally grateful to Dr. Sandberg and to God for everything they have done for

Brandon. Even Efrem has changed into a new person (somewhat). He doesn't yell at the refs as much as he used to. Brandon has an older brother, Efrem, Jr., and suffice it to say he's picked up where his father left off.

Heritage Again

In all of the times we've played against American Heritage, they lost each match up except for one. Kenny didn't play in this game (so it doesn't count...ha!). Tonight, we meet them again, and as always, the venue had to be changed to accommodate the crowd. The last time we met them, there were over 3,000 people in attendance ... for a high school game! This time was no different. We won, but Efrem and I are so upset tonight. On Breakdown's team, three kids play for American Heritage, and of course, Brandon is at Pine Crest. Efrem and I couldn't believe our eyes when we saw the Breakdown brothers sitting at the bottom of the bleachers cheering for American Heritage and booing Pine Crest! Huh? Don't they have kids on their team from both schools? This combined with the arguments, heckling of kids, and lack of supervision on trips has pushed us over the edge. One thing is for sure, Brandon will not play for Breakdown this year!

LaSalle

I will never forget the game we played tonight. Tonight, we played LaSalle for the Regional Championship. As usual, my cowardly self was posted up outside talking to the security guard. Every time I went inside, Pine Crest was on the ropes. We trailed the entire game. With three minutes left, we were down by eleven. The fans from the opposite side were running up and down the aisle yelling, "We are going to the 'ship, we are going to the 'ship!" Coach B called a time out, and all I could see was Efrem standing in the middle of the huddle. Huh? In the middle of the game he jumped down from the bleachers and joined in the huddle! Well, as the story goes, everyone was looking down because they had accepted defeat. Knowing that this would be their final game for the season, Coach B told me Brandon looked at him and said what time is practice Monday? After that time out, Brandon went on an 18-point run! Eighteen points in three minutes! All I know is that the LaSalle fans looked shell-shocked!!! Pine Crest on the other hand went bananas. What a night! No, what a KNIGHT!!!

Back in the 'Ship

What a year! Brandon misses three months because of the surgery and comes back to lead his team to a state championship! Once again, Pine Crest are State Champions. We all went out to dinner after the game, and as usual, Brandon remained his nonchalant self. Efrem goes, "Look happy, man. You are a two-time state champion." Brandon simply replied, "No big deal. I've won two national championships, too!" Ha!

Gatorade

Today was an incredible day. While sitting at home, I got a call from the Pine Crest Athletic Director (AD). Brandon is Gatorade's National Player of the Year! Brandon knows he's the player of the year for the state, but he has no idea he's the NATIONAL player of the year! Right after talking to the AD, a woman from

Gatorade called to tell us that they are coming to Florida to have a dinner at a restaurant for 30 family members and friends and then have a press conference. I'm so excited until I don't know what to do!

***

Later tonight is the Gatorade dinner. Brandon still has no clue about being the national player of the year or the dinner. I swear it's killing me not to say anything. If there's one thing I can't do, it is keep a secret! Many of our family and friends will be there including J.R. who has remained in Brandon's life since his rec league days. T.J. will be there along with a bunch of people from the school as well.

***

We told Brandon that we were going out to dinner and it took him forever to get dressed. He's so slow. He's very slow. It took everything in our power to get him to the restaurant on time. When we finally did get to the restaurant, one of the Gatorade staff members pretended to be the hostess. She led us to a private room, and everyone yelled "surprise!" the minute we walked in! Brandon was floored. During dinner, the Gatorade staff instructed everyone to tell a funny story about Brandon. It was no surprise that not too many people were able to fill their request since Brandon is usually so serious. One of his teammates, Trey, told a story that I don't think I'll ever forget as long as I live. Trey said that one time he forgot a book and came back to the gym to get it long after everyone was gone. In the gym was Brandon sweating and working out as hard as he could. Trey said he asked Brandon why he works so hard. According to Trey, Brandon simply replied ... to be the best. I think that sums up Brandon in a nutshell. He strives for perfection on the court and in the classroom simply to be the best. The dinner has long been over, but I'm still sitting here swelling with pride.

On a side note...in July, Efrem, Brandon, and I will be flown to L.A. where they'll announce the Athlete of the Year. Afterwards, everyone will attend the ESPY Awards. I love Gatorade. They are simply awesome, and they can really throw a party to boot! Who pays for the bar tab these days? Who? GATORADE!

***

Last night was a blast and so was today. Pine Crest is awesome! For an hour, they shut down the school. They told the kids that they were having an assembly to present sports awards. Cameras were all over the place, and of course, the kids tried to pry the secret from the cameramen. Coach Beckerman started the assembly by passing out awards to the team for winning the State Championship. Next, the Gatorade staff took the stage and revealed a banner with Brandon's name and Gatorade Player of the Year. THE PLACE WENT BANANAS! After all was said and done, the press did interviews, and we took Brandon and his friends out to lunch. What an awesome couple of days! Gatorade ROCKS!

Post Season

The post season has more than compensated for such a horrible start. Brandon has received all kinds of honors. He's Mr. Basketball for Florida. He's Broward County's Player of the Year (he was last year, too). He's received several academic awards, and he's closing in on the record for the all-time leading scorer for the county. I'm so proud of him...but I'm most proud of the fact that he's managed to maintain a 4.3 GPA. Brandon rocks!

Florida Elite

(Spring 2009)

A friend of ours introduced us to the owners of this new team, South Florida Elite and we decided to let Brandon play with them. I'm not feeling this team at all. We really haven't gotten to know any of the parents, and to put it mildly, something just ain't right. As with all things, time will tell.

Now I Know
It's been a month with this new team, and now I know what's not right. Reportedly, the owner of the team receives money when Brandon shows up at different tournaments. I don't know if it's true or not, but I do know that everyone was fired up last week when Brandon decided not to play in the Bob Gibbons tournament this year. Reportedly, Bob Gibbons himself threatened not to vote for Brandon to go to the McDonald's All-American Tournament if Brandon doesn't play at the Gibbons tournament! Things are really crazy right now. We can't even sit in peace at a game. The last time we played, about five strangers sat next to us trying to strike up a conversation with us. Everyone is pushing a college, and if they're not doing that, they're trying other angles in order to put money in their own pockets. Basketball is big business. Its cutthroat and only the strong can survive. Everyone is hoping to latch on to the next big thing, and there are plenty of people who are banking that Brandon is THE

next big thing. Imagine being stalked by people looking to latch on to a kid? It's to the point that we don't know who's genuine and who's not. I'm exhausted, truly exhausted. People say we've been spared a lot of the madness because a lot these "street agents" are afraid of Efrem! I have to believe they are. There are many people that come to us but there are many more who take one look at the mean mug on Efrem's face and do an about-face. I knew that sourpuss face would come in handy one day!

Sparks and Flames

My mama always said, "If there's a spark, watch out for a flame." Efrem and I have followed her advice. We've decided to leave this team. We don't know if the accusations are true, and quite frankly, we don't want to know. We just want to disassociate ourselves should these people not be on the up-and-up. We have worked hard to ensure that Brandon's reputation is sparkling, and nothing and no one will ruin our efforts if we can help it.

Each One Teach One

(Summer 2009)

After such an awesome year, it's hard to think about AAU basketball. But, alas, it's summer, so we must. Efrem and I have decided that Brandon is done with Breakdown and the Florida Elite team. Brandon has decided that he wants to work on his body, his shot, and his game in general. Together, we decided that Brandon will only do a few events this summer with T.J.'s team Each One Teach One (he changed the name from the Dream Team). Brandon's senior year starts this year and we need to think about college. We plan on doing our official visits this summer. For once, I'm looking forward to AAU. The schedule isn't as rigorous as last year, so let the summer begin.

Nike Tournaments

Each One Teach One plays mostly in Nike tournaments. Brandon has known most of these guys for quite some time (including Austin Rivers, son of Doc Rivers) and has managed to fit in quite well even though he has only played in a couple of tournaments so far. Today, we played in Virginia against an Ohio team. We had them on the ropes until Brandon hurt his hip. Shortly after Brandon left the game, one of the kids broke his leg. I mean really broke his leg. You could hear the crack clear across the gym. I hate when kids get hurt. I always cry.

I Can't Believe It

We received a call from Ohio State today. Apparently, they were recruiting the kid who broke his leg. But how come they called us and said they really like Brandon and would love for him to come to Ohio? It hasn't even been a week since that poor kid broke his leg, and they are already looking to replace him. Huh?

And So It Ends

Today, we played in the Nike Peach Jam in Atlanta, and Brandon hurt his foot and had to leave the game. I asked the trainer if it was broken because I know Brandon, and he will try to play on it. She told me that if it was broken, there was no way he could play. He walked out of the gym on crutches. We'll see what tomorrow brings. If it's swollen or looks bad, we will take him to the doctor.

***

There's nothing worse than being on the road with a medical emergency. This morning, Brandon's foot was swollen, and he couldn't put any weight on it, so we took Brandon to the doctor, and sure enough, it is broken. To make matters worse, we are supposed to leave here and fly to L.A. for the Gatorade Player of the Year Awards. Brandon looks totally disgusted. We called an ortho doctor in Florida, and after reviewing the x-rays, he said as long as Brandon wears the boot, he will be fine until he returns to Florida. He's probably going to have to have a screw put in his foot. Ugggh!

81

Gatorade Athlete of the Year
Going through security at the airport is hard. Going through security at the airport with a boot or any other device on is downright difficult, which Brandon found out today. Brandon is making the best of his time in L.A., but I know he's not as excited as he would be if he were not weighted down with the boot. Gatorade has a bunch of activities planned, and tonight, we're going to a restaurant/bar/bowling alley. Tomorrow is the luncheon where they'll announce the Athlete of the Year award and tomorrow night is the ESPY awards. There are a lot of kids here, and all of them are great athletes. Brandon is a junior, and everyone else is a senior. I don't want to tell him, but I doubt if he's going to win Athlete of the Year, but that's just my thinking. I hope he does win, but he already won Player of the Year as a junior, and that's unheard of. Only Lebron James and Greg Odom and Brandon have ever won Player of the Year as a junior. I don't think anyone has ever won Athlete of the Year as a junior but I'm hopeful nonetheless.

***

Everyone had a blast bowling last night. We met many of the parents, and they were all great. The luncheon was awesome. Stuart Scott from ESPN announced the winner, and a football player won it for the boys, and a basketball player won it for the girls. I'm not upset; it was an honor for us to even be here. I'm hoping that

Brandon will get a chance at the award again next year. Well, on to the ESPYs tonight. I'm looking forward to it!

***

The ESPYs was fun last night! During commercial breaks, they had a bunch of entertainment, and best of all, we got to see a lot of professional athletes and stars! All of the Gatorade kids got to walk the red carpet, and they were really pumped up about it. The parents got to walk the red carpet also but nobody had a clue as to who any of us were. The crowd just kind of ignored us until the next big star passed along. Poor Brandon had to maneuver the place with the boot on. He had one pant leg tucked in his boot until I told him he looked like a pirate. Ha!

No AAU More Basketball

Who would have thought that Brandon's last AAU game would end with a broken foot? Oh well, such is life. He had surgery last week on his foot and will be out for four weeks. Since he'll be off to college next summer, his AAU basketball season is officially over. Believe it or not, I'm going through basketball withdrawal! Seriously, there's nothing to do for the rest of the summer! Our lives have revolved around basketball since Brandon was eight, and eleven years later, here we are at the end of summer basketball. I never thought this would have had such a profound effect on me. I never dreamed I would miss the gyms and all of the travelling. I guess I'm feeling salty because I'm realizing my boy's growing up, and next year, he will be gone. Next year, he'll be a man. I hate clichés, but wow, time flies!

Recruiting 101

We've tried to postpone this as much as possible, but unfortunately, the time to pick a college is among us. Letters have been arriving in the mail forever. There's an entire closet worth of envelopes to witness to this fact. Still, Brandon has acted like none of this exists, and we've contributed to that. We've insisted that he enjoy playing basketball in high school and to not give college a thought until his senior year. Well, the time is here. At least he's narrowed down his list. So far there's UConn, Kentucky, Duke, Florida, Miami, Kansas, and Syracuse. Starting next week, the coaches will start coming in for the home visits. Can't wait! I have my friend on standby with snacks. I'm the ultimate hostess, and I really want this to be a great experience for Brandon.

First Insult

I think I just handed out my first college insult! Last week as I was on my way to my friend Keisha's house in Tampa, a reporter called asking a bunch of questions that I was in no mood to answer. Among his questions were what colleges were on Brandon's list. I named everyone but Duke! I mean, come on. I'm on my way to hang out with my girl! Who can remember such things! Well, I think Coach Mike Krzyzewski took this to mean Duke wasn't on Brandon's list. He called to express his concerns, and I assured him that it was purely a mistake. Well, Coach K. ended up calling to cancel his home visit with us, and today, Kyrie Irving announced he would be going to Duke. Oh well, guess Brandon was never meant to go to Duke anyway! Duke's loss. Ha!

UConn

Everyone knows that Brandon has wanted to go to UConn forever. Tonight, Coach Jim Calhoun came to visit. I will never forget his opening line. He said, "Brandon, I'm not trying to be your friend. I've known people for 30 years, and they are my friends. Not you." In my best Scooby Doo voice, I had to say, "Rut Rooo!" I found this to be hilarious. Brandon, of course, just looked at him with no readable sign on his face whatsoever. I can't help but think that Brandon was saying to himself, "I don't want to be your friend either." Ha! If that comment were not enough, he also said, "I think Corey Joseph is the best point guard I've seen. Brandon, I would probably play you at the two spot." Huh? This man is NOT saying ANYTHING we want to hear!

Kansas

Kansas came to visit today. Coach Bill Self's opening line was as follows. "Brandon, I didn't recruit you, and quite frankly, I don't deserve to be here." Huh? So I had to ask him that if he didn't think he deserved to be in my house, why was he there? I think he was surprised that I called him out. He gave me a line of crap (which I don't even remember) and went on with his presentation. I don't know if I like him. We plan on visiting Kansas, so I hope I'll be able to get a more discernible read on his character.

Syracuse

By now, I know the drill. They come in, introduce themselves, say no to my snacks (ha!), and then get on with the "Why Brandon should come to my college" speech. After that, they play a DVD that shows their style of play. Next up is some time to chit-chat, and then they leave. Today was no different except for the fact that there was no foolishness. These guys are older men who are all about business. I liked them, but truth be told, I also like a good laugh. But the "Orange Men" offered none. They are strictly about business! There's one thing that's going to sway Brandon from this school and that's the COLD WEATHER. If Brandon decides to go to Syracuse, he's going to rack up frequent flyer miles because he's going to need to come home to thaw out his butt! Ha! Upstate New York is no place for a Floridian. Brandon feels a bit of loyalty to Syracuse, Duke, Florida, and Miami though because they've been watching him forever. Time will tell where he goes.

Kentucky

I really like Kentucky, and everybody knows it. Why do I like them? I like them simply because they were the only college to reach out to me as a parent. When the other colleges make their allotted NCAA calls, they call Brandon himself. However, the coaches at Kentucky took time out to call all three of us, Brandon, Efrem, AND me. With that being said, Kentucky followed the same routine: talk, presentation, blah blah blah. There was one little change to the routine, however. They ate some snacks! Ha! My impression of Coach John Calipari is that he's a cool cat. I think he's slick, but then again, I think all college coaches are slick. Whether Coach Cal is the "Point Guard King" or not, I don't know. I do know that's his reputation, and if there's one thing I know, it's this: Perception is 99% fact in the public's eye!

Florida

We all like Billy Donovan. He's the only coach who knows Brandon. He's been watching Brandon for a long time, and he knows exactly what makes him tick. If I were to say where Brandon is leaning right now, it would be towards Florida. Kenny Boynton is there, and they've been playing together forever. In addition to Kenny, there's a group of kids who are at Florida who Brandon knows. It would be just like going to Pine Crest or playing with the Eagles or Breakdown. But Efrem and I want Brandon to go to the school that's most beneficial to him and not where he's most comfortable. The road to excellence is not always smooth. Sometimes you've got to take the less paved road to your destination.

Miami

Our friends from The University of Miami came to visit today. We've seen Miami at Brandon's games forever. Both Efrem and I love Coach Frank Haith, and we love the staff at the University of Miami. How nice would it be if Brandon went to college right here? UM followed the same pattern as the rest of the visiting colleges with their speech, presentation, and a "see ya later." I can't help but feel a little pressure. At some point, we're going to have to tell all but one of these coaches that Brandon decided not to go to their school. Ugggh!

The decision on which college Brandon is going to attend will be a tough one. Ultimately, it will be his

88

decision. Both Efrem and I have decided that we don't want to sway him in any particular direction. Should things go sour (and I pray they don't), we don't want Mr. Man looking at us crazy. Brandon, begs to differ, however. He's told US to make the decision!! He trusts my input on the academic side and his dad's decision on the basketball side. Not sure that either of us want THAT much trust! Hmph!

Official Visits

After completing the home visits, Brandon has narrowed down his choices to the following: Kentucky, UConn, Kansas, Florida, and Miami. Now it's time to set up official visits to the colleges. Over the next month or so, we're going to try to squeeze in all of our visits. I'm actually looking forward to visiting the schools. I'm excited, and I think I'm the only one who is. Brandon acts like he couldn't care less!

Kentucky
The NCAA has determined that each recruit is allowed to be on campus for 48 hours during an official visit. I swear it seemed like a clock was ticking in the background the minute we arrived on campus today. We toured the facility, went to a tailgate party, attended a game, went to the Coach's house for dinner, and finally back to our hotel. Talk about a whirlwind! The tailgate party and the game were a blast this afternoon. This place is crazy! And the fans are even crazier! Brandon got up to go to the concession stand and about 1,000 people started chanting his name! It seems everywhere he went people were asking him for his autograph. I mean, people have been asking for his autograph since he was nine, but it's been just a few here and there - never a whole crowd at once. I don't know if he'll be able to handle all of this, he's a shy guy. It's too much!!!

UConn
Brandon likes UConn, so we're here. Coach Calhoun tried to clean up his statement regarding Brandon at the

two spot, but truthfully, I didn't want to hear it. I believe he meant what he said and said what he meant. On another note, our trip to Kentucky has taught us a lot. Do not let these people run you ragged. We have no desire to go through the whirlwind that befell us in Kentucky, so we told the coaches that we were not going to the football game they had planned for us to go to earlier this afternoon. We did, however, tour the facilities. I was not impressed with their basketball facilities, but they did say they were building a new one...good! Later in the afternoon we went to Coach Calhoun's house for dinner. He lives in a secluded and heavily wooded area. He seemed to be proud of the fact that bobcats make an occasional appearance on his property. Efrem was not. When presented with this detail, Efrem kindly informed Coach Calhoun that he'd be going back inside!

Kansas
Today, we're headed back to Florida from Kansas. Efrem really likes Kansas. Brandon likes Kansas as well. But as for me ... ehhh. I can't say that I'm on board. My job is academics, and I love their academic advisor. I guess my issue is with Coach Self. I just can't get over the fact that he's never really seen Brandon play. How can you claim you love a kid so much, but you've never seen him play? I just think it's a bunch of foolishness. However, I can say their facilities are the best we've seen. Brandon loves the trainer – a woman! Kudos to her for gaining the respect of all of the coaches! Coach self did, however, tell me that I was the best dressed mom that ever graced the Kansas campus. Maybe I can squash this mother's intuition because of that—NOT! At the end of our visit,

91

Efrem pretty much told Kansas to welcome their newest point guard. So, I guess like Dorothy, we're going to click our heels three times and wake up in Kansas!

Florida

I love Coach Donovan and so does Brandon. Efrem is a different story. Efrem seems to feel Brandon's game will not fit in with Florida's style of play. He also feels Florida is "guard heavy," and Brandon will be hit with a lot of personality problems. We went to a basketball game yesterday, and there were not a lot of fans in the audience. Another thing that we noticed was this: Florida is a football school. All of the money goes to football. You can tell that's where the money goes simply by looking at the facility. The football facility/offices look like a palace. Meanwhile, the basketball facility leaves a lot to be desired. We did get a chance to meet Tim Tebow. At first I was not thrilled. I mean, couldn't they have found something else for us to do? But I must say that meeting Tim was a treat! What a well-mannered young man. I wish him nothing but success in whatever he does, and I really wish I could have met his parents so that I could congratulate them on raising such a fine young man.

Miami

Double my sentiments regarding Florida when it comes to the University of Miami. Miami is a football school, too. There's not a whole lot of support for the basketball program, and we just don't want to plug Brandon into this type of system. Brandon is at Pine Crest, a small, private school not known for sports. I think he deserves to go to a college that's rich in tradition when it comes to basketball. I love Coach Haith, and I love the University of Miami. Nothing will pierce my heart more than having to tell Coach Haith that we've decided to send Brandon somewhere other than Miami. Nothing will break my heart more than saying the same thing to Coach Donovan, but in the end, it's about what's good for Brandon. This recruiting business is tough!

PINE CREST SENIOR YEAR – 2009-2010

How exciting is Brandon's final year? Unfortunately, it's not exciting at all. The Kenny vs. Brandon thing is over. Kenny has gone on to Florida, which ended all of the hype around Pine Crest's season. The fans are still around but not as heavily as last year. As with all things, the excitement surrounding Pine Crest vs. American Heritage is over. *Sigh*

It Ain't Over

Well, after practically handing Brandon over to Kansas on a silver platter, things have gone awry. It seems they wanted an announcement ASAP. We decided not to make an announcement until after the season. Two months have passed since our last discussion with Self, and we haven't heard from Kansas since! I guess it was a case of announce now because we don't believe Brandon is coming. Well, if there's one thing to be said about the Knight family (actually there's a lot to be said), it's this: We won't be forced into ANYTHING! That being said, we're back to square one.

Regional Finals

This basketball season has been uneventful, but tonight was different. We played in the regional finals tonight at Glades Central, which is in this little town called Belle Glade (had no idea it was that small) about 45 minutes from Ft Lauderdale. Glades Central is best known for their football players, and several of the University of Miami's football players came from Belle Glades. Once

94

we got to the school, I knew it was going to be "off the chain." People were lined up outside of the gym to get in. A barbeque grill was fired up in the parking lot, and folks looked like they were going to the club instead of a basketball game...I mean high-heeled gold shoes and all! Once I saw the players, I just knew our boys were going to be intimated. The crowd was hostile, and I do mean hostile. People had smuggled liquor into the game, and you could tell they were tore up. The Grey Goose was definitely flying at Glades Central! When it was all said and done, Brandon scored 48 points! He shot the lights out of the gym!!!! I've never seen an entire school turn against their own team. People were cheering every time Brandon hit a basket. One guy got down on the floor and started rolling around when Brandon hit a half-court three. Another man walked on the court when Brandon was shooting a free throw and told him he'd give him $200.00 if he hit 50 points! At the end of the game, security had to escort the team out of the gym, and everyone was lined up outside giving Brandon high fives. Of all of the games he's played so far, this and the game against LaSalle, will be two games that I'll never forget! As a result of tonight's win, we are headed to another state championship.

The Final 'Ship

A whistle blew, and just like that, Brandon's high school career has ended. We lost. Brandon suffered a pulled groin and couldn't contribute much. I really wanted him to go out with a bang. There's sadness throughout the land. Pine Crest had chartered buses and practically shut down the whole school in anticipation of a huge victory.

But now, our little Pine Crest kids are heartbroken. Shoot, I'm heartbroken!! But what can you do? I sat in the stands and stared at the court for about five minutes trying to take in the fact that Brandon will never play in another high school game again. I wiped a lone tear from my eye. So long Pine Crest.

The Decision

Today is the day Brandon announced his college decision. Boy, am I glad this is over! It seemed everywhere we went, someone else was asking us where was Brandon was going. I was sick of it. I mean, I was really sick of it! One of the teachers at Pine Crest said Brandon was walking past the playground where the little kids play and was bombarded with the magical question, "WHERE ARE YOU GOING?" The teacher said she hasn't seen Brandon go to his car via the playground again. Ha! Well, in the end, we chose Kentucky. Kentucky is rich in basketball tradition, the fans are bananas, and we really wanted Brandon to experience a place where the fans loved basketball. I feel like he made the best choice, and as a family, we're happy with the final decision.

On another note, Pine Crest shut down the upper grade levels for a period, and everybody gathered in the auditorium. The media was there, and they even had the band on deck! Coach B looked like he was about to choke. Ha! He's from Connecticut, and he loves Connecticut. I know nothing would have pleased him more than to see Brandon go to Connecticut, but we just didn't feel that's were Brandon needed to be. When

Brandon said the University of Kentucky, the auditorium went crazy. There were even some Kentucky fans in the audience! What??? I feel like a 100-pound weight has been lifted off my shoulders. Maybe people will leave us alone for a minute. I know things are about to go crazy, but I just pray Brandon will relax and enjoy the rest of his senior year. GO CATS!!!

Player of the Year
Once again, Brandon has made Gatorade's Player of the Year!! Now, Brandon has been up for a lot of post season awards. He's won some, and he's lost some. Had he lost this one, I would have simply passed out! I love the Gatorade staff and events. This is Gatorade's 25th anniversary year, so they're going to be doing things a little differently from last year. This year, they're going to surprise Brandon in his classroom. Alonzo Mourning will be presenting him the award. I can't wait!

What a Surprise!
Today was the best day, ever! This morning, we all met at Pine Crest for the Gatorade award presentation. While Brandon sat in his class, all of our family members and friends lurked just outside the door. The teacher told the class earlier that Alonzo Mourning would be doing a lecture on the globalization of basketball. Alonzo began speaking but after about three minutes he went to a cabinet and presented Brandon with the Gatorade Player of the Year trophy! Next, everyone, including camera crews, walked in. Very rarely is Brandon rattled...today was one of the very few occasions I've seen him about to blow a gasket! After the classroom presentation was

over, all of the high school kids went to the auditorium for a press conference and celebration. The festivities ended tonight with the Gatorade dinner. Everyone we invited came out to show their love and support for Brandon, including his neurosurgeon and his orthopedic surgeon! All of the Pine Crest staff members spoke about what a joy it was to have Brandon in their lives for these past few years. Every staff member we came into contact with at Pine Crest told us what an exceptional son we have. I, like them, will hate to see Brandon walk away from Pine Crest for the final time as a student.

Mr. Basketball

Although Brandon won Mr. Basketball last year, the Florida Dairy Farmers Association didn't present the award to him formally due to scheduling conflicts. However, this year was different. Everyone knows how I love Gatorade, but this presentation had to be my favorite. I loved it because the school decided to let the little kids attend the event for a change. Truth be told, the high school kids were taken out of school three times on account of Brandon, and I think it was getting old. After all, these parents aren't paying $18,000 a year to have their kids attend Brandon's awards ceremonies. Ha! Anyhoo, for the first time, the kids in kindergarten through fifth grade got to attend something. The place was absolutely bananas! There was a person in a dancing cow costume getting groovy on the stage, and word got around that it was Brandon dressed up as the dancing cow! Now, I know that would NEVER EVER happen in a million years, but they didn't, and those poor babies spent a half hour screaming for Brandon to come out of the cow costume! When nonchalant Brandon finally did come in through the main auditorium doors (he was taking a test), I thought the roof would cave in from the noise. After the presentation, the kids wanted autographs, and after Brandon signed a few, the Athletic Director told them that was it. Brandon told the Athletic Director that he had a free period and stuck around to sign everything for everyone. It's days like today that he makes me extra proud. No kid left without an autograph or a picture. Way to go Brandon!

All Star Games

The all-star games are among us. Let me just say I hate all-star games. I always have, and I always will. For starters, it's all about showing off. Nobody plays defense, and everybody hogs the ball. This is where kids know they're being watched, and they do everything within their power to make sure they get their 40 minutes or so of fame. Brandon never does well in any all-star situation. He tries to play the game correctly (it's the perfectionist in him) and refuses to hog the ball and throw up shots. Truth be told, I'm not looking forward to any of this! Ugggh!

USA Games

This year, the USA games were held in Portland, Oregon. I've been to Portland once, but this time is different because we have time to explore. Today, we went to the beach, and it was absolutely beautiful. These types of events are usually packed with things to do, but the USA Games are different because there're not a lot of things planned for the parents. Tonight, however, we did go to a Trailblazer game, and tomorrow, the kids will play their game. The Trailblazer game was exciting. We sat in a suite with the kids and the other parents and pretty much got to know everyone. I'm bugging Terrence Jones's mom terribly because I really want him to go to Kentucky with Brandon. I'm keeping my fingers crossed!

***

Brandon didn't stink up the place, but he wasn't one of the "show boaters" either. The game was exciting, and Brandon did what a point guard is supposed to do: run the team. The USA team won, and afterwards, they had a buffet-style dinner in a room under the arena. It was a fun event, and it really gave the parents a chance to get to know each other. I met Kendall Marshall's parents and Harrison Barnes's mom, and we had some very nice conversations. I'm so proud of all of the kids. God bless them all!

McDonald's All-American Game
This year, the McDonald's All-American Game is being held in Columbus, Ohio. The only thing good about being here is the fact that my sister lives here. Ha! For the most part, we have no access to our kids for the week because they're busy doing charitable events and going to places of interest in the Columbus area. We've seen Brandon in passing while at the hotel, but that's about it. Tonight is the three-point contest and the slam dunk contest. We've been trying to get Brandon to enter the three-point contest, but I don't think he's going to do it. He's a shy guy! Tomorrow is the McDonald's banquet, and I'm really excited about going because the kids will be dressed in tuxedos and gowns. As for the parents, we've been asked to dress formally. Can't wait!

***

The banquet was fabulous! It was held at the convention center in a huge room, and the boys looked so handsome, and the girls were beautiful. In the beginning, the boys escorted the girls down a set of stairs while being introduced. Once everyone had been introduced, the kids were able to go around the banquet hall and mingle. There were carving stations placed all over the room as well as areas for side dishes and desserts. Hundreds of people were there, but there were no lines at any of the buffet stations. Go figure! After the mixing and mingling came the presentations and some awards. McDonald's did an excellent job. Tomorrow is the game.

***

Well, tonight's game had its pros, and it definitely had its cons. Let's start with cons. The cons: Brandon stunk! Ha! No, really, he stunk! He didn't play well at all. He missed several shots, and he just didn't look like himself. He did, however, hit the winning shot! His team was down by two, and he pulled a three from his bag of tricks. As I've said a hundred times before, Brandon's thing has never been all-star games. But it is what it is. And if I know one thing about Brandon's future, it's that he will drop in the rankings, and that's because it's all about points and finesse. Jack up a lot of shots and create some moments for a highlight reel, and you will move up in the rankings when all-star games are played. Oh, well. At least he's headed to college now. Who cares what these high school ranking services think? I hope Brandon doesn't.

Jordan Classic
The Jordan game is in New York City, and who doesn't like visiting New York City? Tonight is our first night here, and we went to a dinner at a local banquet hall. I had a ball! The centerpieces were different Jordan shoes encased in glass. John Sally was the M.C., and it was just a very fun-filled event. There was a DJ, a hip-hop violinist, and a comedian, and everyone had a ball. By now, all of the parents know each other, and some of us have become friends. I love Terrence Jones's family! Whether they come to Kentucky with us or not, I'll always keep in touch with them. They are so much fun! Well, tomorrow is the game. Let's just hope it goes better than the McDonald's game!

***

Not a good game for Brandon tonight. There's talk of him slipping in the rankings already. Oh well, this is it. The last whistle has blown, and high school is officially over. On to Kentucky!

The Aftermath
Rumors can really circulate fast, and they have made their rounds during the course of the all-star games. Several parents said they've already seen the names for the MVPs written out prior to the McDonald's game even being played! And some parents have even claimed the same held true for previous all-star games as well.

What??? Everyone knows that the MVP is selected based on the number of points a player puts up, and rumor has it that once one kid has started passing the player who has supposedly been selected as the MVP, the coach pulls that kid out of the game so he can't pass the MVP's point total. I do know that Jared Sullinger was the high scorer in one game, but he did NOT receive the MVP award. I really hope these things are on the up-and-up. I mean, whatever you do, especially if you're a major corporation sponsoring a game, BE FAIR!

On another note, Brandon slipped in the rankings from the #1 spot to the #6 spot. I think he's okay with it. As for me, it stings that he's judged on three games, but that's the nature of the business. It is what it is.

Graduation

Today was a very bittersweet day for me. What a joy to see Brandon graduate Summa Cum Laude, but oh, what pain to know this is it! No more high school games, no more living at home, and no more watching this boy eat food and drink Gatorade at an alarming rate. I cried. But hey, what's a mother to do? As a parent, this is a day that you look forward to. But now that it's here, it's hard. I know I should be jumping for joy that Brandon has not only finished high school while earning straight A's the entire time, but he's going to college on a basketball scholarship. He's also going to enter college with 22 credits because of the advanced placement classes he's taken. I know this should be a joyous occasion, but it's not. I feel sad because deep in my heart, I know life will never be the same for any of us. Sigh.

Another sad but true fact is this: I will miss Pine Crest! I must admit I had my reservations at first. I mean, Brandon was one of very few African Americans attending the school, and I worried that he wouldn't fit in or be accepted. Nothing could have been farther from the truth! Brandon could have been the mayor of the school! What a great feeling to have just about every teacher and administrator come to me to tell me what a wonderful young man he is! When Brandon was in the eighth grade, the local newspaper did an article on him. I think the photographer summed up the Pine Crest culture very well when he captured a six-foot-tall Brandon walking down the hall with a little Jewish kid, who was only about five feet tall, eating pizza. I will never forget the kids, the staff, or the coaches at Pine Crest. Happy summer to you all, and to all, a good-bye! Sniff, sniff.

Go Big Blue

(Summer 2010)

Today is the big day. Today, I'm taking Brandon to college. We're catching a flight since his car was shipped with all of his things piled in it. I asked him if he was nervous, and he admitted that he was. Poor thing. I think the unknown is what has him leery. I, on the other hand, am excited! I'm kinda feeling like I did when he entered high school. I was like, "No more junior high! On to bigger and better things!" And I feel the same way now. No more high school! On to bigger and better things! What a change from a couple of months ago when I cried because he was graduating. We've been reading the message boards, and everyone is excited about the upcoming year in Kentucky. I can't wait!

First Day on Campus
I'm exhausted. I have spent the entire day running to and from Wal-Mart. Sheets, TV, towels, etc. Brandon's room looks really nice. I decorated it pretty well for him, and I'm hoping it's going to be a comfortable place for him. For all of the things that are great and wonderful about Brandon, there's one thing that isn't. HE IS A SLOB! No, I mean, he is a SUPER SLOB!! I have no delusions that his room will not look like it's been hit by an atomic bomb in another week.

***

Brandon met with the academic advisor, Mike Stone, today and has been put on track for his classes. I've told both Mike and Brandon that I'm not trying to see a degree in basket weaving. I really want Brandon to major in engineering, but everyone is saying that it's just too difficult to do while playing basketball. Hmmm, I bet Brandon can do it. There's been kids who have gone from Pine Crest on to Harvard, Yale, and Stanford, and they've all said the same thing: PINE CREST IS HARDER! So pursuing an engineering degree while playing basketball at Kentucky should be a piece of cake!!

John Wall, John Wall, John Wall
If one more person compares my baby to John Wall, I don't know what I will do! Today, some guy from Sports Illustrated called, and the first thing he said was, "Brandon has some pretty big shoes to fill. I don't think he realizes whose footsteps he's about to fill." Huh? Sir, have some class about yourself! We're talking about a 19-year-old kid. CUT HIM SOME SLACK! If that's not enough, every message board, blog, and whatever else folks use to communicate with these days are constantly comparing the two. John Wall is a great basketball player. He's proven himself. Give Brandon a chance to prove himself as well, and THEN start the stupid comparisons if it's absolutely necessary. Better yet, enjoy them both and stop it. Who would want to step into this kind of pressure?

What?

When Brandon decided on Kentucky, rumors were raging regarding Coach Cal going to coach in the NBA. To prevent Brandon from being stuck with a coach who didn't recruit him, we decided to have Brandon sign scholarship papers only. This way, Brandon will have a loophole to leave should things turn sour. W-e-e-e-e-ll, today somebody called me from the Lexington newspaper, the Herald Leader, and I am still reeling from this call! The first thing this guy asked me was, "Who told us about signing scholarship papers only?" What? I'm totally insulted. To me, this question implies that we're ignorant people who could not possibly have enough sense to read the rules for ourselves. Ever since Brandon got jammed up with the Jammers, Efrem and I have been very careful not to get crossed up again. It's every parent's responsibility to know the rules of engagement. We slipped once, but never again. When I informed Mr. Reporter that nobody had to tell us anything, we simply read the rules and saw the loophole, he stuttered and hung up the phone. The nerve of him!!!

Gatorade Athlete of the Year

We met Brandon in California for the Gatorade Athlete of the Year Awards. As always Gatorade put on a spectacular event. We are staying in an art deco type hotel in California which is practically attached to the Staples Center. After attending all of the events, today was the luncheon and Brandon Knight is officially the Gatorade Athlete of the Year! Once again Stuart Scott made the announcement. Lisa Leslie was there and we took lots of pictures with her and her husband. Lisa's husband came to congratulate us and tell us how articulate and well-spoken Brandon is. He said it really made him proud to see such a class act…GO BRANDON!

UK Basketball Season – 2010-2011

Windsor, Canada

Today was a wild and crazy day! I knew the Kentucky fans were crazy, but geez, I didn't know how far the insanity reached!! As we approached the gym today, I was shocked to see that a sea of blue was standing in line! Kentucky fans are in Canada?? Wow!!! I had a chance to meet a lot of fans before the game started. Apparently, somebody discovered we were+ Brandon's parents. Well, word traveled quickly, and the Kentucky fans swarmed to the area in which we sat. Kentucky fans are the BEST!!!

During the game I met this one elderly gentlemen whose name is Darryl. He promised me that this team will go deeper into the tournament this year than the team did last year. I got his number and told him that I would be calling him when tournament time approached to see if he was still standing by his claim. On another note, we won the game with no problem! Brandon looked great, but this team was not any real competition. I am very curious to see how he measures up against some tough competition.

Still no word on Enes Kanter. This is a major bummer. One of the main reasons that we chose Kentucky is because we thought we were going to have a big man to be reckoned with. Something's got to give. If we don't get Enes, we are done! I pray that the NCAA will be swift with their decisions.

111

***

Brandon flew back to Florida with us since this will probably be his last time home until Christmas. Overall, the tournament was fun. I'm anxious to see what the season brings. I was glad that I met some of the parents. I got a chance to meet Jon Hood and Darius Miller's parents along with Jared Polson's dad. They seem like a great bunch of people. Jon Hood's mom was especially helpful. She pointed out some of the diehard fans and showed me the ropes as far as meeting Sandy Bell, the compliance person for tickets prior to games. Everyone seems to be excited that Brandon is a Wildcat and I'm grateful for all of their help.

Cut Me Some Slack!
Can somebody please cut me some slack? I plan on moving to Lexington to be near Brandon for his first year. There're a lot of adjustments, and I just want to be sure that he's okay. There's only one problem. The NCAA! Everybody is tied to UK in some way in this town, and therefore, it's hard for me to get a job. I found a wonderful place to live, but guess what? The owner is affiliated with UK! This is going to prove to be more difficult than I imagined. It irks me that people are making money hand over fist from these kids, and a parent can't do something as simple as get a job without worrying about the ramifications. I mean I'm no idiot nobody would be GIVING me a job. I'm a writer, I worked as a systems analyst for over 15 years, and I worked in employee benefits at Aetna for a number of years. You would think I would be an asset to any company...ha!

I digress...getting back to the unfairness of everything. During the tournament in Canada, I saw someone with a shirt on that said, "I got a feeling tonight is going to be a good KNIGHT." The person who made the t-shirt is making money from my and Brandon's last name. OUR NAME! And get this, we will never see a penny of it. There has to be so many rights that are being violated. How does any organization get the right to dictate if an owner of a company can hire an individual simply because he/she loves his/her football/basketball team? How can they dictate when or how I use MY last name? What's more, how can they dictate who a person can lease their private property to? THIS SUCKS!

Midnight Madness
Tonight was my first night ever being in Rupp Arena during an event. Tonight was Midnight Madness. I can't believe it. I simply cannot believe it! Thousands of fans were at this event, and it wasn't even a game! We knew UK was rich with tradition, and we knew the fans were bananas, but I had no idea!

Midnight Madness was a blast! When the players were announced to the crowd, the kids came out and did some funky dances. It was pretty funny stuff. Efrem and I had no clue what Brandon would do - but we knew for sure that it wouldn't be dancing! If there's one thing that Brandon can't do, it's dance. I remember when he was seven, and he asked me for money for a dance at the Girls and Boys Club. I told him I didn't want him dancing because I didn't want anyone making fun of him. He looked at me and said, "I know. I'm not a dancer. I'm an athlete!" Well, tonight he remained an athlete. Brandon simply did a little salute to the crowd and kept it moving.

On another note, the girl's coach stole the show. This man came out and did the Dougie! I mean, he did it right! He had swag. GO COACH MITCHELL!!

In Hot Lex
Who would have ever thought I would be living in Lexington, Kentucky? I met my girlfriend, Keisha, at work many years ago and when she told me that she was from Kentucky I laughed. I laughed because I had never met an African American person from Kentucky! For years Keisha and I have been going to the Macy's Music Festival in Cincinnati and we always stay with her mom in Lexington for a few days before and after the festival. In all of these years I would have never guessed Lexington would someday be my home. Well, as of today, I am officially a Kentucky girl! I finally found a job and a place to live. I initially found a place over a deli and I must admit that I was pretty excited about it. Efrem, Efrem, Jr., J.R., and I arrived in Lexington last week and after one look at the deli apartment, Efrem Jr. said, "Aint no way my daddy is going for this!" True enough, Efrem Sr. took one look at the place (which wasn't cleaned or painted) and said, "There's no way I'm staying here." He then proceeded to tell me, "Tonya, there's trash cans loaded with food out back and therefore there's going to be 'food rats' in that apartment!" For some reason Efrem thinks he's a rat

expert. According to him there are: Food rats, field rats, wall rats, flying rats, and river rats (to name a few). After much debate I relented and told the owner that we didn't want the apartment. I'm an eclectic chick and that was really an eclectic place but in the end the "food rats," settled the dispute. We then went to a loft that I looked at on a previous trip to Lexington, and settled on that. Efrem just looked at me and shook his head while saying, "What is wrong with you? How could you choose that other joint over such a nice place like this?" I just looked at him and rolled my eyes while wondering if there was a way to keep the "food rats" out of the other place…ha!

Maui

Last night, we arrived in Maui. I know I keep saying this, but it needs to be repeated. UK FANS ARE CRAZY! We got here around midnight local time. The hotel lobby was empty, and after a 12-hour flight, all we wanted to do was get to our room and get to sleep. We did that, and this morning when we got down to the lobby, I was literally shocked. As far as the eye could see, there was a sea of blue! Wildcat fans were everywhere! There are thousands of fans in Maui! In Maui!!!

***

I've been hanging with Terrence Jones' mom and aunt as well as Doron Lamb's mom while here in Maui. Tonight we made plans to go to the Jacuzzi; Efrem says he hopes there's enough room in the Jacuzzi for all of us

"Golden Girls," since the jacuzzi is tiny (or is it because we're a little "juicy" in the hips?). I've been examining this statement very closely and I still haven't found any humor! Since arriving we've been getting a kick out of the fans. When someone finds out one of us is a "Wildcat Mom," we quickly point to another mom and say: "There's Doron's mom, or there's Terrence's mom, or there's Brandon's mom." The fans get such a kick out of meeting us. Who would have ever thought we'd be celebrities. We've taken pictures, signed autographs and met some really great friends. Tomorrow we play UCONN.

***

Tonight we played UCONN and it was a disaster. Let me repeat…A DISASTER! I stayed outside and got updates via phone from friends and family in Florida. Terrence's aunt, Ava, came out for smoke breaks to give me updates as well. During the half Ava came out and looked at me and said, "It's bad, real bad, Tonya." She wasn't lying, it was a blood bath.

As a parent you want to do something…anything to make things better. Unfortunately, there's nothing that I can do.

***

Overall, this was not a good tournament for Brandon. As a matter-of-fact, this has been a horrible tournament for Brandon. I've NEVER seen his confidence shaken this badly. Efrem and I prayed with him, and as parents, we let him know that we believe in him no matter what. There's a lot of pressure on these kids regarding this one and done business. We made it clear to Brandon that he'll get to the NBA eventually and not to worry about how long it takes. We told him to not feel pressured and to just go out and play. I think he's a little confused with the offense and Coach Cal's style of play. We're in paradise, but we feel like hell. After this last game, Brandon looked at us and gave US a pep talk (go figure). He said, "Stop worrying. I'm a smart kid. I'll figure it out." Unfortunately, this tournament is going to haunt him for a long time in the media. We had a long talk with the coaches, and they told us not to worry, he'll be fine. I pray that he will. He's got a long road ahead of him.

***

It's Thanksgiving Day and we're just getting back to Lexington after a day of travelling...a twelve hour flight combined with a seven-hour layover in Seattle. We left Maui around 12 p.m. yesterday and had a chance to chat with Doron Lamb's mom before leaving. We had a ball laughing about our AAU days. Doron played on the team that had the fan with the cow head costume (The New York Gauchos). He was the fella that told us basketball players came from New York and football players could be found in Florida. While we were talking, Doron's mom reminded us about one of our feuds in which she called one of the Breakdown moms "Black Beard," (because she had a beard). I had totally forgot about that one. As I recall, that exchange almost ended in another fight because "Black Beard" was fired up! Looking back at the AAU years had us cracking up. When I think about the seriousness of college basketball I hate to admit it but I long for the AAU days. I hated to leave but we had to go. I can't wait to see my "Golden Girls" in Lexington.

We flew into Cincinnati and guess what? A sea of blue flooded the airport. It seems everyone got back around the same time. I saw some of my new friends from Maui and promised I would call them once things got settled. I really had a ball with a lot of the fans and can't wait to hang out with some of them soon!

Whose Side Are You On?
I've vowed to stop reading the message boards. After the Maui trip, I discovered the fans can be a great thing, and they can not necessarily be a great thing. Brandon is taking some brutal punches by his own fans! I understand that some people are posers and are probably just on the board pretending to be Kentucky fans, but I know some of these people are UK fans. People can be cruel. We release our children into the hands of these fans to love them and support them, not to belittle them when things go wrong. The mother in me wants to get on the internet and tell everybody off. The rational adult side of me simply says to let it go. It literally breaks my heart to read the mean things that people say. Yet, when I'm out and about, I get so much love from the fans so I have to believe the internet posters are the minority—not the majority. I've talked to several people, and they

have assured me that the people posting on the message boards represent only a few true blue fans.

First Game at Rupp

Tonight, we played our first regular season game at Rupp and won! Most people think the parents get a lot of special privileges but we don't. We must find parking like everybody else! We do, however, occupy the first four to five rows behind the home goal. Prior to each game we must meet the compliance lady, Sandy Bell, and sign for our tickets. Guests must sign that they haven't paid for the tickets, etc.

I can't describe the pride that I felt when Brandon was announced, and everyone cheered for him. I know there are some fans who have thrown him under the bus, but I have to agree with everyone else. These people are outnumbered by fans who love him. Brandon played well tonight, and he looked like himself on the court. In my heart, I know he's going to be just fine. "The Golden Girls" have gone back home but the Miller's, Polson's and the Hood's are still on deck. Mr. Hood is so passionate. He sits in his seat intently watching the entire game. The Polson's are really kindhearted and fun people. They cheer the team on even though their son doesn't get much playing time. Mr. Miller, on the other hand, is the life of the party. He rallies the troops (us parents) and cheers the team no matter what happens. Mrs. Miller is quiet and laid-back.
Overall, the first season game was awesome, something I'll never forget.

North Carolina

Today we played North Carolina and lost. There's a ton of fans in my building. I left out of my place and went to wander around in the hallways while the game was on because of my nerves. As it turned out, I could have stayed where I was. I could tell what was going on based on the yells and awwww's coming from each door! When we were up everyone screamed, when we were down, the awww's prevailed. In the end, we lost. I can't stand losing so I'm going to blame it on the refs. THEY CHEATED! Hopefully we'll see North Carolina again. At least I know where the true blue fans live. Maybe next time I can join one of their parties. It should be simple to get in; I'll just tell them I'm Brandon's mom! Ha!

Louisville

Oh my. Nothing could have prepared me for the UK vs. Louisville matchup. This is serious, I mean real serious. This is worse than the Pine Crest/American Heritage rivalry. I started to make the trip to Louisville but decided to go to The Big Blue Martini and watch the game locally. I'm really glad I did because I met a new friend. As I was walking in the room I asked if "we" were winning to this woman who was watching the game. She calmly looked at me and said, "It depends on who WE are." Turns out she was rooting for Louisville! A couple of people started talking to me and she gathered I was Brandon's Mom. She came over and introduced herself to me. Her name is Elaine and she's the superintendent for Clark County Schools. She told me how impressed she was with Brandon's academics and asked me if I could get him to come out and talk to her students one day. I assured her that I would get him there. We exchanged numbers and decided to meet up for lunch one day. Elaine's husband and son are UK fans and we won so I guess I can befriend a Cardinal....ha!

On the Road Again

North Carolina, Alabama, South Carolina, Ole Miss and Florida, all losses. I hate to lose!! I wake up the next morning covered in the agony of defeat. Kenny Boynton is at Florida, and he finally got his chance! If anyone had to beat us, I guess I don't mind that it's Kenny. The fans are really coming down hard on this team. First of all, there's only a six-man rotation. Secondly, the point guard has to play the entire game. Third, it doesn't look like Kanter will play. It's just bad on so many levels. Real bad. To top things off, Calipari has been riding Brandon really hard. Coach Beckerman called me and said he hates to see Cal yell at Brandon. He said Brandon is an intellectual and yelling at him is not the way to get results....I totally agree.

Today, I called Calipari and he said, "Yes, I'm in his a*%, but he will be okay." I wanted to tell Calipari to get out of his a*% and maybe he'd get better results, but figured I'd keep my mouth closed because if Brandon found out I called Coach Cal, I'd be in serious hot water. Getting jazzy with the man would only take it to the boiling level. Brandon would really pop a spring! But I did speak with Orlando (the assistant coach), and I told him my opinion on how to get through to Brandon. I told him Brandon is a very intellectual and analytical person. I told him that playing psychological games with him wouldn't work because he will only analyze what you tell him and discredit you if he decides it's foolishness or untrue. I told Orlando that dancing around in Brandon's head is not a good idea—he functions better when a person is straight to the point with him. Orlando thanked me for my insight and then he told me something that I will never forget. He said, "Miss Tonya, if it were easy, everyone would be doing it." And Orlando is right. I remember when Brandon won the Gatorade Player of the Year. They said he beat out over 500,000 kids playing basketball in the country. Just think, of those 500,000, only a few will go on to a D1 college. Even fewer will make it to the NBA. Brandon's dream is to go to the NBA. Because Brandon wants it, I want it for him. As a mom I want to pave the road with jelly beans and gum drops even though I know it's unrealistic. I just wish there was something that I could do short of marching down to Cal's office and throwing a temper tantrum! COACH CAL, LEAVE MY BABY ALONE!!!!

The Hyatt

I love attending home games. Before each game everyone gathers at The Hyatt for drinks/dinner/snacks. I usually go to The Hyatt before games and I have a ball! I've meet some more friends (who drive down from Louisville) and they save me a seat. The place is a madhouse but it's a blast! I've met a ton of people at the Hyatt and their affectionately known as "my Hyatt friends." Tonight I met a woman who had to be the jazziest seventy-year-old ever. I don't know why but there was just something about her that made me want to be around her. I told her as much and she invited me over her house to watch the next away game…I'm going to go too! Well anyway, we played Tennessee and won. It was hilarious because the kids kept yelling barbeque at Bruce Pearl (referencing his troubles with the NCAA for allegedly having an illegal barbeque at his house).

Mississippi State

As usual I met my "Hyatt Friends" prior to the game and had a ball. This time Elaine (the Louisville fan from Blue Martini) joined me! Elaine and I have become fast friends. I just love her. That being said…Elaine has sworn that she'll be a UK fan as long as UK is not playing against Louisville. I guess I can live with that! Hahaha! Elaine's husband and son, who are die-hard fans are a little jealous because she was with me at the game. They called her an imposter…ha! Brandon hasn't had a chance to go talk with the kids in her district but he told me as soon as things calm down he told me he'd be there.

During the game tonight the kids were teasing Renardo Sidney one of the Mississippi State players. Apparently they thought he was a little chubby and decided to call him "cheeseburger." Although I wasn't near the visiting bench I could see him looking back in the stands while mouthing off. I was later told that he spent the majority of the game cussing our fans out! Although I missed that episode, I'm glad my "Dancing Man" showed up. During every game there's this guy that slides up and down the rail and dances his tail off whenever they play that song *Mony Mony*. Tonight, the "Dancing Man," all decked out in his UK gear didn't disappoint. I saw him after the game and asked him if I could dance with him at the next game. He looked at me and said, "Sure honey, come on!" Gotta love UK Fans!

Florida

Tonight was our home game against Florida. We won! Yaaay!! The Golden Girls are here and we're going out tomorrow and I'm inviting them over for dinner on Sunday. Some of Brandon's Pine Crest friends flew down for the game and we went out to dinner at P.F. Changs. As usual, it didn't take long for fans to gather enough courage to come over to our table of eight and request pictures/autographs. Brandon is a good sport and has become very patient with kids. On our way out we saw Terrence Jones eating with his family while signing autographs. Gotta love the Big Blue Nation!

On another note...our team is looking good, and despite what the naysayers spit out, I feel confident that we will be okay in the SEC Tournament. After the games the parents are allowed to wait for the players outside of the locker room. While we waited for Brandon, I ran into Kenny Boynton in the hallway. He looked kinda' down, so I went over to him and gave him a hug. I told him that he has nothing to hold his head down about. Kenny was a warrior when he played at American Heritage, he was a warrior when he and Brandon played with Breakdown and he is a warrior now that he's at Florida. I wish him nothing but success (except when Florida plays Kentucky)!

SEC Freshman of the Year

I'm heated. I'M REALLY HEATED! Today, I found out that Brandon didn't get SEC Freshman of the Year despite every poll in America voting him as the SEC Freshman of the Year. I learned that Coach Calipari made his nomination based on a coin toss between Brandon and Terrence Jones. I love Terrence, don't get me wrong, but whatever you do, do it because you believe in it. Had Cal nominated Terrence because he felt he deserved it over Brandon I would have been fine. But, the fact that my son has been reduced to a coin toss is insulting to me. Brandon couldn't care less, but I do. We didn't toss a coin between Cal and Billy Donovan, Coach Haith, or Coach Calhoun. We choose Calipari based on what we felt were his merits. I could go on and on about this, but I'm tired. My head hurts, so I'm going to bed.

***

Coach Orlando sent me an email this morning saying that he hopes I feel better. Well, I don't. I replied with an email of my own telling him that I didn't feel better. In fact, I told him that the only thing I felt was betrayed. I love Orlando, and at some point, I'm going to have to squash this and apologize to him. Orlando has been nothing but helpful from day one. After all, Orlando didn't toss the coin. As for Cal ... humph!

125

SEC Tournament

OMG! Atlanta is filled with blue. This is crazy! UK fans are crazy!!! They are even offering discounts at bars for UK fans to draw in a crowd. I'm so excited about the game tomorrow. I CAN'T WAIT! The Golden Girls are here but we haven't had a chance to meet up. I'm excited because I'll get a chance to see them tomorrow at the game.

**

We played Alabama today and won. Woooweeee! Afterwards, we gathered in the lobby with a bunch of my Hyatt friends as well as some of my other friends that I've met while in Lexington. Well, as we were sitting around chatting guess who sits with a group of people across from us? Bruce Pearl! During the recruiting process there were hundreds of letters sent to us from Tennessee. The envelopes all have a picture of Bruce in his orange jacket pointing. Since those envelopes have been the source of much laughter in my house, I had to introduce myself. I said, "Mr. Pearl, I'm Brandon Knight's mom and I just have to shake the hand of the man who's responsible for all of those envelopes coming to my house." He laughed and said, "Too bad you didn't get the right one." All of the UK fans just burst out laughing. Considering all of his NCAA woes, I think Bruce should have kept that comment to himself. Can you say barbeque, Bruce?

***

Alabama yesterday and Ole Miss today! I knew my baby was going to be just fine. He's broken several UK records, and he's playing great! I'm still a wuss. Everyone says I've wasted my UK tickets and should give them to someone else. I've spent both games in the lobby talking to the security people!! (By the way, they're really nice). Yesterday when I decided I was leaving, Mr. Miller blocked my path. He said, "Nope, you ain't leaving today." I finally gave him the slip and I was out...there's no keeping me in a gym I've had several years of experience. I'm a smooth criminal! Most of the parents just look at me and shake their head. The Polson's just look at me and crack up laughing. I usually return to my seat sometime around the end of the fourth quarter and yell GO UK! The parents usually boo me. Ha! Well, on to Florida tomorrow for the championship!

***

SEC Champs! Whooo hooooo!!!!! Although I go outside during the games, I do, however, peep at the scoreboard from time to time. As the clock began to wind down today, I ran to my seat (all decked out in my #12 jersey with my face painted) and started screaming. Once again, I got booed by the parent section! I love it! And I loved watching each and every parent look out on the court with a smile on their face. We stayed after everyone left and the boys came out and gave us hugs. Our boys have taken a beating in the media and many people didn't think we could do it, but we have. Terrence Jones' mom summed it all up. She said, "Ha! They don't know what our boys are going to do in the NCAA Tournament!" GO CATS!!!

March Madness
Now I know why they call it March madness. I'm mad! We got the worst seed that we could possibly get. I don't know why folks hate Kentucky, but they do. In order to get to the championship, we are going to have to go through some tough teams, Ohio State (number one ranked) among them. I'm nervous, but I have faith. Our boys have swag about them these days. I think they smell victory! I called the elderly gentleman, Darryl, that I met in Canada and asked him if he was still sticking by his claim that we would go farther in the tournament than UK did last year. He got the greatest kick out of hearing my voice. Even though he kinda waivered because we didn't get Enes, he said he was still standing by his claim. I'm going with what Darryl says over any of the sports analyst. Ha!

***

We played Princeton today. I stopped by Harry's and watched the game on the patio with a ton of UK fans. I really thought we were going to blow past them, but we didn't. For a minute, I thought we were going to be haunted by the road-loss ghost. Brandon didn't have a great scoring game, and things were looking pretty bad. But our boys held it together, and out of nowhere,

Brandon scored his first two points of the game, at the buzzer, giving us a win! HOW ABOUT THAT?!?

***

Today I met Elaine, her husband, Al and her son Ryan at the Hyatt to watch the West Virginia game. Ryan is what one would call a "True, true, blue fan." No matter how many we go down by Ryan has faith that we will win. I told Ryan that he's the guy that you need when you're in the trenches. The Hyatt was packed and for the most part I was able to sit still and watch the game. That's not to say that I didn't have my moments when I had to get up, but overall Ryan was the glue that held me together. Towards the end of the third quarter Ryan simply looked at me and said, "Ms. Knight, sit down and relax…WE GOT THIS!"

***

The great Ohio State went down today like a puff of smoke!! The sports world is shocked. Nobody expected Kentucky to come out of this game victorious. Oh well! So long Ohio State! Brandon is being known as Mr. Clutch. He didn't have a great scoring game, but again, he hit the game-winning shot. I love it! Our boys are the greatest. My sister lives in Columbus and said that people are joking that they are going to put a hit out on Brandon. Seems to me Brandon put the hit on them! Boy, are we executing revenge!

***

I work with this kid who turned out to be a double agent! I had planned on giving up my tickets to a game so that he and his wife could go. But, due to friends coming in from out of town, etc., I never got around to it. Thank God I didn't! Just prior to this game I found out he is an Ohio State Fan! When I saw him at work today I couldn't help but rub it in his face. He looked at me and had the nerve to say, "I bet they shut Brandon down!" Huh? What? Well, after that comment I had to blast him. I said, "Too bad they didn't shut him down at the buzzer!" I then said, "I'm so glad you didn't get one of my UK tickets. I would have felt like a real sucker right about now!" Ha!

The Day Before the Final Four

Okay everyone, it's almost here, and it's stalking me like an alligator does the foolish who decide to fish in the Florida Everglades. But unlike the Foolish Florida Fishermen, I know my foe is licking its chops, and I can do nothing but sit and wait for it to descend upon me and devour me slowly - bit by bit. What's this monstrous thing that's harassing this Basketball Mom, you ask? THE FINAL FOUR!!!

As each hour draws near, my heart migraine (a pounding headache in my heart) worsens. This can be only be attributed to two things: not wanting to lose this weekend and the pressure of not packing enough Kentucky blue outfits to wear! Losing would be a tragedy, but not representing the Big Blue Nation in proper fashion would be absolutely catastrophic! How can I ever surpass the gentleman who showed up at the Maui Invitational in the checkered blue and white pants? Or the fella with the Kentucky blue flashing-sunglasses? Or the woman with the blue and white wig?

Some say we'll win, and some say we'll lose, but make no mistake about it, I want to win!! But should we lose (God forbid), and I find myself laid out on an ambulance stretcher from the stress of it all, I'll be the jazziest basketball mom at the game! How can I be so confident, er, arrogant? This basketball mom has just discovered that she's packed a three-outfit per game wardrobe change!

I know somebody's got to win, and somebody's got to lose, but everybody can't be as jazzy as a true blue fan!

GO BIG BLUE!

The Day After

If the refs hadn't cheated, we would have won. If Brandon wasn't tired, we would have won. If Calipari would have called a time-out at the end, we would have won. And, as my mother used to say, if a frog had a glass behind, it would break because he hopped on it too much. That is what happens when you live in the land of ifs!

The fact of the matter is we lost, and we are going home without the trophy. It hurts. To top things off, the UConn fans are hanging out in our hotel lobby harassing the UK fans, and that hurts even worse. (I'd like to hurt a few of them, but that's probably illegal in Texas. I should check and be sure.)

Hurt hangs in the air around this city filled with UK fans like a hovering buzzard above a dead carcass. All we true blue fans can do is give a half-hearted smile as we pass each other going to and fro. Unspoken words linger, but they never find their way past our lips. Perhaps it's because nobody knows quite what to say.

Regardless, my beloved Wildcats made it to the Final Four, and that's more than everyone but UConn, Butler, and VCU can say.

To all the boys in blue, I salute you for a great season and for providing us with great memories. Shelve your uniforms for a couple of weeks and trade them in for jeans. I know you're anxious to get back in the gym to work on perfecting your game for next year, but try to relax for a few days if you can. You deserve it!

GO BIG BLUE!

The Announcement

I feel like I did last year when Brandon was about to announce what college he'd be attending. Everywhere I go, I get asked the same question: Is he leaving? As of right now I honestly don't know. This is a very difficult decision for a 19 year-old to make. There's a lot a stake and whatever decision Brandon makes will be a life-altering one.

I do know that Brandon will not make any decisions until Coach Cal has some teams come out to look at him. Once Brandon works out for some of these NBA teams, and get Coach Cal's input, he'll have a better chance of figuring out where he fits in the puzzle.

***

After much discussion, debate and agonizing, Brandon has decided to enter the draft this year. It wasn't until Coach Cal told him that he no longer had a scholarship (meaning he should go to the NBA) that Brandon made his final decision. There's only one thing that Efrem and I require, and that's for him to finish college. Since he's almost classified as a junior it shouldn't be that hard for him to take online classes and complete his degree. I've been bombarded with questions about our feelings regarding Brandon's decision since we are big on education. My reply is this, "If you could do the thing that you've dreamed of doing for your whole life while making millions of dollars doing it, what would you do?" I haven't met a person yet who told me they would

134

pass and finish school. Whatever decision Brandon made, Efrem and I wanted it to be his. We don't need Brandon to take care of us; both of us have worked all of our lives and will continue to do so.

After the announcement, I did something that I vowed not to do again...look at the message boards. Many people congratulated Brandon but, oh boy, there were many fans that trashed him. One person even said, "All these one and done kids do is use Kentucky." Huh? College basketball is a multi-million, if not billion dollar a year business. My son averaged playing 37 minutes (I think) the entire season. His body got very little rest and he gave 100% every time he stepped on the court. For that, he didn't receive a dime even though Rupp Arena was packed every game. Sure the powers that be hide under the guise that he received a free education. But seems to me if he and his teammates packed a gym for every home game, during the SEC Tournament, the Sweet Sixteen, the Elite Eight, and the Final Four, they paid for that scholarship a million times over. How dare anyone say he used Kentucky?

At the end of the day, the good far outweighs the bad. I've met some wonderful fans whom I've grown to love. I really do believe that the supporters far outnumber the bashers. I will miss the games at Rupp, I will miss the fans, and most importantly, I will miss the dancing man who slides up and down the handrails every time they play *Mony Mony*. I don't know what it is about the Big Blue Nation that sucks you in...all I know is that it does. I will always and forever BLEED BLUE!

The Coaches

Even though I don't agree with all of Cal's tactics, I have to bow to the fact that Brandon respects him a great deal. Brandon once said, "He's the greatest coach in the world!" I have no regrets regarding Brandon coming to Kentucky. At the end of the day Cal got Brandon to where he wanted to be and for that I will always be grateful. Who knows maybe one day me and Cal will sit down together for a steak dinner (his treat of course) ha!

Coach Orlando has been my rock during this crazy year. When things would get rough he was always around to lend an ear and offer encouragement. He also cracks up at my antics. I think he especially gets a kick out of me and my girlfriend, Keisha's, claims that we are: Respectable and upstanding ladies. Whenever Orlando talks to me he always finds a way to say something or somebody is respectable and upstanding. He then cracks up laughing.

Coach Strickland is another rock. He always provides feedback as to how Brandon is doing and how hard he works. I like him because he's honest. BOY IS HE HONEST! When we were in Maui I looked at him after Brandon's performance against UCONN and asked him if it was bad. He looked me straight in the eye and said, "Yeah, it's bad!" Thanks a bunch, Rod!

Coach Payne has always believed in Brandon's abilities and has always let him know that he was great.

Sometimes that's all a kid needs to keep pushing towards greatness.

Coach Newton has gone on to another school and I miss him already. Although every coach at some time or another has come to me or Efrem and told us that we did a great job raising Brandon, Coach Newton has expressed this about Brandon to us on many occasions. Coach Newton is responsible for making sure the boys do what they're supposed to do. He once said, "If all of them were Brandon I wouldn't have a job. Your son just does the right thing....always!" Before leaving UK Coach Newton told me that he was a better person for having met my son. Thanks Martin, that meant a lot to me—there is no greater compliment to a parent.

The Draft

I'm just getting home from the draft, and it's been a whirlwind. This basketball mom is tired! Limos, champagne, fancy dinners. What's a basketball mom to do?

Seriously, the draft has made its way on my list of "Most Stressful Things in My Life." From the minute I arrived in New York, I got caught up in a tornado that didn't stop twisting until I touched ground back in Lexington.

Approximately one hour after arriving in New York, we had to attend a parent/player meeting. Apparently, the NBA has a developmental department. Huh? I thought it was the just the NBA. You mean to tell me they have *departments*? There are about ten people in the Developmental Department, and their job is to make sure rookies transition into the NBA well. "Who's moving with him? Can he cook? Will he finish school? Does he have a girlfriend?" These were the questions fired off at us in a span of ten minutes. I honestly felt like I needed a lawyer! At the end of the meeting, they smiled. I guess we "did good."

The meetings/activities did not stop. A *mandatory* parent meeting was scheduled for later, bowling, dinner with Brandon's agent, a briefing on *green room* rules, etc. etc. etc. Perhaps the most interesting meeting was the NBA Basketball Mother's club/organization (not really sure what they call it). Who knew?

It wasn't until 2 hours before the draft the following day that all of the mandatory meetings finally finished. We immediately had to rush to get dressed and run outside to our chartered buses, which took us to the draft in New Jersey. Meanwhile, during all of this madness, we received news that Brandon was tumbling in the draft from the #3 spot. Talk about stressful!

Fast forward to the green room (which is nothing more than the floor of the arena with black carpet and tables). As we sat at the table and Utah didn't pick Brandon at #3, I wanted to pass out. However, the fear of being put on Sports Center, sprawled out on the ground with my legs gapped open, prevented me. To add to the stress, Calipari sat next to me (I should probably make an effort to get over the tossing of the coin incident). My friend Avis asked why I didn't smile. I had a very simple reply for her: There was nothing to smile about!

As names were called, the tension mounted. Finally, Brandon's agent got a phone call from Detroit around the #6 pick. "He's going to Detroit," Arn, Brandon's agent whispered! "Whew! I can finally breathe," I thought. Calipari looked at me and smiled. I wanted to roll my eyes and turn my head, but I had just been given a gift from God, so I thought it better to not tempt fate, so I smiled back. "If they pick him at 8, I will even hug you!" I said to Calipari. He laughed.

Finally, David Stern came from behind the infamous curtain and said, "At the #8 pick, the Detroit Pistons select ... Brandon Knight!"

What followed was a period to exhale. All of the AAU games, high school games, and college games had led to this moment. This basketball mom had done her job and delivered her baby into the hands of the NBA, something that he'd dreamed of forever.

Diary of a Basketball Mom

Kenny and Brandon (the hairdo that he hated from the Boost Mobile game)

Just a few of Brandon's trophies

More trophies, plaques, and McDonalds All-American Jersey

The Pine Crest Cheerleaders

Gatorade National Player of the Year (Alonzo Mourning and Brandon)

Gatorade ceremony in the auditorium at Pine Crest

Walking the red carpet at the Gatorade Awards

College announcement

Posing at Pine Crest

Me, Efrem and our Suma Cum Laude graduate

McDonalds All-American banquet ("The two Efrems" and Brandon)

McDonalds All-American banquet (me and the fellas)

Me in Maui....smiling on the outside and crying on the inside

Party in Maui

First game at Rupp

The ultimate warrior (Ohio State vs. Kentucky)

My UK Office (notice I only hang up clippings about Brandon!)

Me and Elaine goofing off with the Cat.

Me and my second favorite "baller" in the world, Kenny Boynton

Me and some of my Hyatt friends

SEC Champs!!!!!

Computer screen of a Basketball Mom...can you say THREE?

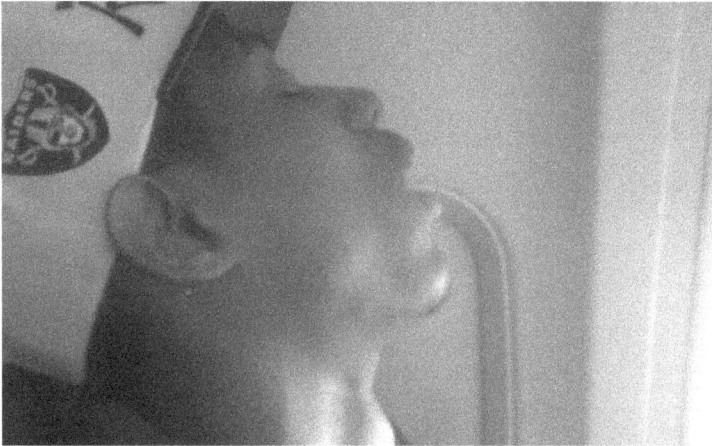

I love taking these pictures (on the way to Florida after the Final Four)!

At the draft.

First pitch at the Detroit Tiger's game

An Official Piston

www.ingramcontent.com/pod-product-compliance
Lightning Source LLC
Chambersburg PA
CBHW052008090426

42741CB00008B/1604